Mother Knows Best?

Mother Knows Best?

The Truth About Mom's Well-Meaning (but not always accurate) Advice

Sue Castle

Skyhorse Publishing

ACC LIBRARY SERVICES AUSTIN, TX

Acknowledgments

First and foremost, I thank my husband, Jay, for all the time he spent in doing research, writing, and editing as well as coming up with some great "old sailor's tales." The voice "I" in the book really should be "we."

I also appreciate the many suggestions and anecdotes that came from my mother, Sadye Garonzik and her good friends in Gloversville, N.Y. They are as always, young at heart and definitely not "Old Wives."

And then there are all the experts and specialists, too many to list here, from associations and organizations around the country who generously gave the real facts about these common notions.

My final thanks goes to Gail Kinn, my editor, who patiently managed to make sense out of all those packets of OWT's, delivered piecemeal over the past six months.

I dedicate this book to my mother and hope she will take my anecdotes about her in the spirit they were intended, with love and caring.

Contents

Introduction

On a morning news show the other day, referring to the guest's last statement the host asked, "Is that true, or is it just an old wives' tale?" Why so cavalier a dismissal of the received wisdom of the ages? I thought. Are all old wives' tales automatically false?

These questions—and my own predilection to pass along some flimsy advice—stopped me in my tracks. I felt compelled to get to the bottom of things. Is it all just superstition or is there a grain of truth to any of it?

For centuries, the collective memories and wisdom of mothers and grandmothers kept the family going safe, strong, and healthy. Experience being the greatest teacher—another old wives' tale?—taught those, without the benefit of today's "experts," to deal with the forces of nature in the best way they could. My own mother, a major disseminator of such admonitions as "Don't read in dim light, you'll ruin your eyes," wasn't wrong about a lot of things. So how was I to separate what was useful from what was totally hogwash?

But today we do have experts, and I decided to turn to them and others in my search for not only the truth but the story behind how these ideas developed. Join me now in a fact-finding mission and a close look at over 100 of the most well-worn old wives' tales—plus some old sailor's tales, old farmer's tales and some old carouser's tales as well. I trust that afterwards we will all know whether or not to drink one glass of warm milk to get us to sleep.

Mother Knows Best?

1

Don't Cross Your Eyes and Other Things You Shouldn't Do

Don't Cross Your Eyes, They'll Get Stuck That Way.   *Not True*

The thought of going through life cross eyed was enough for me to stop this particular trick. For some reason, maybe because it gets a laugh or will scare your little brother, most kids love to cross their eyes.

Lucky for them, there's absolutely no truth to this warning. In fact, ophthalmologists point out that children who have the muscular control to bring the pupils to the inner corners are probably the *least* likely to have crossed eyes.

The medical term for any condition where one or both eyes are turned abnormally is *strabismus*. Worried parents are told by concerned friends, "just wait and he'll outgrow it." "Not true!" say specialists. When it comes to starting treatment, usually vision therapy, the earlier the better, for psychological as well as physical reasons. We all know that other children can be really awful when encountering even a mildly cross-eyed playmate.

Don't Put Plants and Flowers in a Sick Room. They Use Up Oxygen.   *Not True*

Imagine this . . . you've got a cold. You are awakened in the middle of the night by the sound of someone or something breathing. In a panic, you leap out of bed, switch on the light, and find your house plants inhaling in the corner of your room.

To hear the old wives tales about it, you'd think that's exactly what happens if you're careless and allow these grasping, gasping, greedy greens to suck up vitally needed oxygen from your sickroom.

Although, at our home, we sleep with a number of plants and have never heard them panting in the dark—and could not find one mention of this warning in dozens of home health care books—we decided to check this one out with the New York Botanical Garden anyway. To our surprise, in talking to Maria Long at the New York Botanical Garden, we discovered that many people, in fact, call up to ask this very question. One woman told them she had just thrown out every plant in the house when she heard about all the oxygen they steal. Was such a rash act necessary?

Plants do require some oxygen, says Ms. Long, for the process of photosynthesis. Like animals they metabolize full time, but they only photosynthesize during daylight hours. So even if they were to gulp oxygen by the tankload, they would not do it at night.

Fortunately, plants don't actually breathe—day or night. The photosynthesis process involves so little oxygen that it is insignificant in human terms. As Ms. Long points out, even a human being, sleeping in the same room, will not use up all the oxygen, or even enough to interfere with the breathing of another person in the same room. So how much oxygen could a plant...or plants, use? The answer is nothing remotely significant.

As a matter of fact, not only is this old wives' tale blatantly false, it is actually the reverse that is true. Plants in the sick room can indeed be of some help. According to recent studies, plants aid in the elimination of many air pollutants, especially carbon monoxide.

So don't hesitate to invite a leafy green plant into your home. Not only are they perfectly harmless, but they can go a long way to cheering up a sick person's room. Just check to make sure he or she isn't allergic.

By the way, another common misconception regarding plants is that those with fragrant, colorful flowers are the worst allergy offenders. Once again, the reverse is true. These plants, in fat, propagate by attracting bees, which spread the pollen. They don't discharge pollen into the air. The real contributors to hay fever are the plainer plants and grasses.

Don't Read in Dim Light, You'll Ruin Your Eyes. *Not True*

Since I was a diligent carrot eater, and still became nearsighted enough by fourteen to wear glasses, my mother found another explanation: reading under the covers by flashlight (necessitated by a 9:00 P.M. lights off curfew based on the dictum that "Children need to get enough sleep"...I'll deal with that one later).

I grew up hearing that I ruined my eyes by reading in dim light, although the flashlight was really quite bright.

Now, whether it's psychological or physiological, I have a real aversion to bright lighting. So my children grew up living in a house with adequate but indirect lighting, dimmers, and very few lamps. Aside from the constant complaints that they couldn't see what they were eating, there's no proof it affected their eyes. One child has 20/20 vision, and the other wears glasses only for reading.

Experts support my stubbornly defended belief that this truly is just an old wives' tale, albeit a very popular one. The American Academy of Ophthamologoly assures us, "Reading in dim light can no more harm the eyes than taking a photograph in dim light can harm the camera." The eye muscles that change the focus of the lens aren't "hurt" by dim light; this is *not* the cause of nearsightedness or farsightedness.

However, the eye muscles might get tired if you have to strain to read, and that could cause tension headaches. Besides having adequate light, doctors recommend taking a break after every twenty minutes of reading. Just look up from your book and focus on something fifteen to twenty feet away.

Y ou'll Get Zits If You Eat Chocolate, Fried Foods, Have Sex....   *Not True*

The list could go on and on about all the good things that cause pimples. An estimated 80% of adolescents suffer from zits or pimples at one time or another, so it's no wonder that so many theories appear.

The good news from dermatologists is that all of the above are just old wives' tales. In a study performed at Yale University School of Medicine, teens consumed large amounts of chocolate. Even those who were prone to acne did not show a significant difference. In fact, doctors say that there are no foods that cause pimples—unless you're allergic to a specific food, in which case the allergy shows up as a rash. Since adults can generally eat chocolate and fried foods without breaking out, this is obvious common sense.

Dermatologists also confirm that zits are not a result of sex, lack of sex, masturbation, or exercise. And there's no need to scrub the skin off your face in order to keep your pores clean...no matter what the ads recommend. Dirt and surface oil do not create zits, and a normal amount of washing with mild soap and water is usually adequate.

So what does cause pimples and acne? While the underlying cause is still unknown, genetics may play a role in determining the severity of this common condition. However, doctors do have a clear understanding of the process. Here is a simple explanation.

Hormones, particularly testosterone, increase during adolescence, stimulating the sebaceous glands to enlarge and produce more oil (sebum) in the skin's pores (follicles).

The pore is also lined with skin cells. Normally, the oil and dead skin cells shed by the lining rise to the surface and are washed away. A pimple is formed when the dead cells clog the opening to the pore, causing the cells, oil and bacteria to build up until the pore is infected.

Besides genetics, stress may also play a role in triggering the process that produces acne. This could provide the answer to the eternal question: "Why did I have to get this gigantic zit just before the prom!"

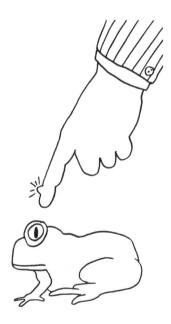

Touching Frogs or Toads Will Give You Warts. *Not True*

I wonder how many millions of children have had their natural curiosity about these amphibians dampened with this dire warning. I vividly recall, somewhere around age ten, playing with a frog and sometime afterwards, watching in horror as ugly warts appeared on my hands. It was enough to convince me that my grandmother knew her stuff. And after all, warts and the bumps on frogs do look very much alike, which is probably why the connection was made hundreds of years ago.

Fortunately for my own children, this misconception was corrected by the time they were old enough to start chasing toads in the garden. According to dermatologists, warts are caused by many different viruses, some of which are easily passed among children. While unattractive, they're harmless enough and usually disappear even without medical treatment, according to their own unpredictable timetable.

Since warts do disappear by themselves, there's a kind of magic to that which makes the situation ripe for the old wives' tales spinners. I don't remember how I did get rid of mine, but thankfully I never had to swing a black cat around by the tail in a churchyard: a remedy popular back in the Middle Ages!

Eating Too Much Will Stretch Your Stomach. In Order to Lose Weight, You Have to Shrink Your Stomach. *Not True*

Millions of dieters believe these are valid explanations for how you gain weight in the first place (the larger your stomach, the more you need to eat) and how you begin to lose weight (you eat less when your stomach is small). Makes perfect sense, doesn't it?

It certainly did to me until I started doing research for this book. The doctor I checked with just laughed and explained that you can no more shrink your stomach by not eating, than you can shrink your lips. The same goes for stretching it through overeating. Now, some desperate, obese people have had their stomachs stapled so they can eat only small amounts. That works, but what a way to lose weight.

While the physiological rationale to these old wives' tales is wrong, there is a reason why they might seem true. When you eat smaller amounts at meals, your stomach produces less gastric acid, so it's less likely to rumble and you can go longer between meals without feeling hunger pangs.

My problem is whether to tell the truth to my husband. After all these years of laying a guilt trip over second helpings at the dinner table, I dare not lose my only strategy for helping him keep his diet.

Eating Too Much Sugar Can Cause Diabetes.　　　　　　　　　　*Not True*

It's true that sugar intake is a serious problem for diabetics. But according to the American Diabetes Association, the condition occurs when the body produces insufficient or inefficient amounts of insulin, which is the hormone that regulates how the body metabolizes sugar.

Sugar does not cause diabetes. What does? Diabetes tends to run in families, so there might be a genetic factor. Also, about 80 percent of people with adult-onset diabetes are overweight, and obesity makes it more difficult for insulin to work efficiently.

If You Don't Stop Sucking Your Thumb, You'll Get Buck Teeth.
Maybe

Dentists say not to worry even if a child's first teeth do protrude from thumbsucking. It won't affect the permanent teeth unless thumbsucking continues when they start to come in, around age five to six. But most children have long since given up the practice by this age. If not, check with your child's doctor about the best way to break the habit...yelling and embarrassing don't work.

Thumbsucking is really a normal instinct. Sonograms

show some babies even start in the womb. Psychologists advise this is a natural way of dealing with tension, boredom and fatigue. Too bad adults can't indulge!

You'll Catch Cold If You Go Out in the Night Air. *Not True*

I'll never forget our first ski trip to the Alps. We checked into this lovely little Austrian *Pension* in St. Anton late at night, so tired from the long train ride from Zurich that we could have slept on a bench. Imagine our joy to find plump comforters and huge fluffy down pillows on the beds, and a massive, friendly armoire in the corner of the room. All was perfect except for the windows, which were not only closed, but doubly sealed with heavy, bulletproof shutters.

Naturally, like all naive Americans, we unlatched them, opened the windows wide, and crawled under the womblike comforters so only our noses stuck out. In seconds, we were dead to the world.

Morning broke with a strange sensation, sunlight and wind. Wind? Upon opening our eyes we discovered snow had drifted in through the windows and almost buried the foot of the bed, while the wind was whistling through the now frigid room. We shivered, not only from the cold, but in anticipation of the reaction of the formidable frau.

We couldn't have been more wrong. Instead of a display of rage, the woman was totally distraught, and thankful. These poor simple Americans had, in their ignorance, let in—and somehow survived—the dreaded night air.

This fear of the night air is a particularly stubborn *OWT* to dispel, especially in Europe. Those quaint shutters that are so much a part of every old building on the continent have given way, over the years, to much more elaborate closures, some of which give the feeling of being sealed up inside a roll top desk.

What is it about the night air that so threatens to cause illness? Scientifically, nothing. Other than the fact that, lacking the sun's warming rays, night air is usually cooler than day air. But that's about the extent of the difference.

So why the shutters? The answer may be found in superstitions, where the night air plays host to goblins and demons and things that go bump. As time went by, scientific reasoning replaced belief in the supernatural, but there was still a degree of subconscious apprehension. Catching a cold, or an unexplained illness, became a seemingly more sensible reason to hide behind the shutters than keeping out the bogey man.

Leaving aside the night air, the annoyance and frustration surrounding modern medicine's impotence in preventing or curing the common cold have given rise to countless other persistent myths concerning the cause of colds, such as ...

Don't Go Out With Wet Hair, You'll Catch a Cold.
Not True

There appears to be real logic behind this. After all, when you go out with wet hair, the hair begins to dry and the water evaporates. And what is evaporation? Right. A cooling process. So going out with wet hair will make your head colder. How does that open you up to the ravages of the cold germ? It lowers your resistance, you say. The same goes for ...

Sitting in a Draft...or...Not Wearing a Hat...or...Not Wearing a Sweater...or...Getting Your Feet Wet..or... Getting Chilled...etc., etc.

This must be true. After all, think of all those movies where someone gets cold and wet, and in the next scene he's sitting with his feet in a tub of hot water and a thermometer in his mouth. People swear they can always

12

put their finger on just such an event before each onslaught of cold or flu.

But, how many times have you become cold, gotten wet, been caught in a storm, been dumped overboard in a lake, shoveled snow, or become cold in a thousand other ways, and *didn't* catch cold? How many incidents of sudden chill have you breezed through in perfect health?

The Common Cold Unit in Salisbury, England, conducted repeated experiments in which people were left shivering in the cold, and did not come down with any more colds than those who stayed warm. Studies done in Texas went one step further. Actual viruses were dropped into the subjects' noses, but exposure to low temperature made no difference as to frequency or severity of colds.

Many other studies, including one done at the south Pole, have supported these findings. The august American Academy of Pediatrics clearly states, "Your child will not catch a cold by being taken outside on a cold, wintry day, by sleeping in a draft, or by having his blanket fall off during the night." Obviously, the same holds true for adults. Chills, even though they are not a cause, can be a symptom or signal that you are already infected and are running a fever. This news really shouldn't be surprising. After all, if getting chilled was a prerequisite to catching a cold, why aren't people in tropical climates cold-free? A friend of mine who grew up in Cuba remembers she was never allowed to go out with wet hair, yet caught frequent colds.

Still unconvinced? Let's look at what modern medicine *does* know about the common cold. First of all, with over two hundred viruses, there's no such thing as a "common" cold. Next, there is only one way to catch a cold—by coming into contact with a cold virus. The good news is once you've had a cold, you're immune to that particular virus. This explains why children generally catch more colds than adults. However, there is no clear explanation for why some people show more resistance to cold viruses than others, who seem to pick up everything "going around."

But why do you tend to get more colds in the winter when you're more likely to get chilled? The answer is simply that's when you spend more time indoors, in closer contact with people and their germs. Even in warm climates, children are in school during the winter months, so they pick up cold viruses and then bring them home.

How are these viruses passed from one person to another? Of course, everyone is aware of the dangers of coughing and sneezing, but new studies show that finger-to-nose contact is the most likely means of transmission. Doctors say the best way to avoid colds is to keep your hands clean, and keep them away from your nose. Now, what about the belief that...

Don't Go Swimming Right After Eating, You'll Get Cramps and Drown.   *Not True*

If there is one rule that has caused more childhood misery than this one, I can't imagine what it would be. I thought my parents were bad when they made me sit on the beach for at least an hour, sweltering in the hot sun, hands sticky with the juice of tomatoes or oranges combined with sand, and gazing longingly at the relief of cool clear water just yards away. But my friend who grew up in Cuba tells us the required wait was three hours in her family. That meant she had to eat breakfast at six in the morning if she wanted to go swimming with her friends. We checked with people from all over Europe who all brought out similar stories.

The pseudoscientific reasoning given by parents went something like this: The blood supply the muscles would normally use for swimming is needed to digest the food. Therefore, the resulting lack of oxygen would increase the tendency for muscles to cramp.

By the time our own children were of swimming age the waiting period had been modified down to a half hour or less. But the concern was still about cramps after eating.

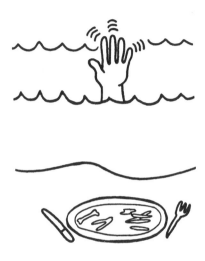

Did all that misery really save lives, or did generations of children suffer in vain?

To find out, we went to the source of all good information about swimming, the people who used to issue the proficiency cards we carried so proudly: The American Red Cross.

Bev Hoover, Health and Safety Specialist at the national office, told us that cramps do occur while swimming. But they have little or nothing to do with how soon after eating you take the plunge. They occur, for the most part, in one of your muscles: either in your arm or your calf. These cramps can be caused by fatigue, cold, overexertion, or simply by being out of shape.

Stomach cramps, which are better defined as abdominal

or gastrointestinal cramps, can result from the same factors. More likely, they can be attributed to overeating, or eating food that may have spoiled from the heat. But these cramps will appear whether or not you go swimming.

The important thing to know is what to do when you get a cramp. The Red Cross says: just relax, do not become panicky or alarmed. Reassure yourself that your buoyancy hasn't changed, and you are still floating. Often just changing your swimming stroke will relieve the cramp. Or, float and massage the muscle. If it's a foot cramp and you're in deep water, take a deep breath, roll face down, extend your leg and flex it, and reach down and massage the muscle.

Often an intestinal cramp will pass in a few moments, especially if you don't get anxious. If it doesn't pass, then get out of the water as soon as possible, again without panic.

Whenever you're at the beach or pool, remember the American Red Cross's "dangerous toos"—too tired, too cold, too far from safety, too much sun, and too much hard playing. But going swimming "too soon" after eating isn't included. If your kids, or you for that matter, want to plunge into the water right after a hot sticky lunch, it's fine. Let's finally leave this *OWT* high and dry on the beach.

Shaving Makes Your Hair, or Beard, Grow Back Thicker. *Not True*

I wonder if the reason European women tend to avoid shaving their leg and underarm hair is the fear that if they do, the hair will grow in thicker.

I still remember the agonizing that went on at teen sleepovers as we struggled with the momentous decision:

did we really need to start shaving our legs, or could we hold off a little longer? We never doubted that the hair would grown in thicker and make us slaves to the razor for the rest of our lives. What we didn't know, my husband pointed out was that teenaged boys have a similar fear.

They're not worried about their legs, of course and they have an almost suicidal urge to get on with the business of scraping their faces—which has become a modern rite of manhood. But they do worry about shaving too high up on their cheeks, thinking, as we do, that the facial hair is going to start sprouting where it's going to be...ooooh, gross!

Well, we can all relax, and shave to our hearts' content.

In *The Skin Book*, dermatologists Arnold Klein and James Sternberg give the reassuring news that there is no truth whatever in this commonly held belief. Shaving an area will *not* make the hair grow back thicker. This really is just an old wives' tale.

They also have something to say about another shibboleth of shaving....

Shaving Against the Grain Will Make Your Hair Tougher.
Not True

During our research we discovered why it was that men began to shave their faces in the first place. Contrary to the popular wisdom that men shave to make themselves more handsome, it seems the practice dates back to the days of hand-to-hand combat. Men shaved their beards because they didn't want to give the enemy any more to grab onto than they already had.

If we must shave, and I refer to men and women both, it is advisable to shave "with the grain." Not, however, because it will make the hair or beard tougher, but because it will prevent ingrown hairs.

Hairs don't grow straight out from the skin, but rather at

an angle ranging from 30 to 60 degrees. If the hair gets cut "against the grain," or against this angle, it is left with a sharp point which can pierce the skin or grow back into the follicle as it curls back; because of this problem it is also not a good idea to shave too closely. Interestingly, this is more of a problem for African-American men because of their naturally curly hair, which can too easily curl back into the follicle.

Drs. Klein and Steinberg offer this sure-fire strategy for men who have a problem with ingrown facial hairs: "Grow a beard." Then just make sure you don't get into any hand-to-hand combat.

Getting Mumps as an Adult Makes a Man Sterile. *Not True*

A few years ago, there was an outbreak of mumps at a school near us, sending all the male teachers into a panic. The first thing they did was put in anxious calls to their mothers asking, "Did I have mumps when I was a child?" The lucky ones who did felt they could rest easy in their immunity. It would have been smarter to call their doctors—but no one thought to question the truth behind the axiom that getting mumps as an adult causes sterility.

In fact their virility was safe in either case. Christine A. Nelson, M.D., in her comprehensive guide *Should I Call the Doctor*, offers the reassuring advice that even "mumps orchitis" (inflammation of the testicles) "is usually a temporary problem and is not (as frequently thought) a common cause of sterility." However this condition is "extremely painful," and even the more usual type of mumps that affects the neck glands can cause severe illness in an adult. So, whether you're male or female, if you didn't have mumps as a child, and you were never inoculated, it's a good idea to get immunized.

Don't Touch Poison Ivy Blisters, You'll Spread It.
Not True

Poison ivy has been tormenting people for centuries. There it is, lurking in the brush, waiting to smear the unsuspecting and afflict them with an itchy, pimply, blistery, fast-spreading rash. We're warned to watch out for "three leaves on a red stem"...a description that happens to fit lots of greenery. So it's tough to avoid this insidious enemy until it's too late, and recognition usually hits when the itchy blisters appear. The reflex is to scratch, and the last thing you want to hear is that you'll only keep spreading it.

Well, there's good news and bad news. The good news is that you can't spread poison ivy by touching (or even breaking) the blisters...assuming you've washed the area so there's no plant resin left on the skin. The belief that poison ivy spreads through the bloodstream is equally false. The bad news: it's still not a good idea to scratch, since broken skin can become infected, making things even worse.

So why do blisters often maddeningly continue to appear on different parts of the body.. for days, even weeks after the first signs? First, there's the strong probability that it wasn't just your skin that came in contact with the plant; it was also your clothing, shoes, gardening tools, etc. Second, if it isn't washed off, the oil or resin from the plant can last almost indefinitely at full strength. Since you may be unaware you've encountered poison ivy (it takes two to four days for the first red spots or blisters to show), the resin could have been spread to everything you've touched. Finally, the spots that appear later may have received a lighter brush with the plant.

So, the question is, is there anything that can be done to stop the spread?

If you're lucky enough to recognize that you've just walked through a patch of poison ivy, wash the resin off immediately with soap and water, or rubbing alcohol. This might prevent any reaction. Then, as soon as is practical, strip and wash your clothing...don't forget to wipe off your shoes. Even after you've started to itch, was *everything* you were wearing or might have touched...tools, steering wheels, etc. If you do all of this (or are sure you haven't been near anything green for weeks), but still break out.. try washing the dog.

That's how to help stop the spread, but what helps relieve the itch? As a child, I can vividly remember taking purple baths! Many parents felt that if gentian violet stopped the spread of impetigo, why not poison ivy? Not true.

Instead, doctors recommend using calamine lotion or cool compresses of witch hazel or Burow's solution. A mild hydrocortisone cream can also be applied on a small area if the skin isn't broken. Extremely sensitive people may need a shot of corticosteroids.

All this advice also holds true for poison oak and poison sumac.

Turning a Light Off Just for a Few Minutes Uses Up More Energy Than It Saves.   *Not true*

I readily admit that I did not inherit this belief from my mother. Whenever she visits me, or more importantly, when we visit her, she always comments on my family's habit of leaving the lights on all over the house. She refused to buy my explanation (even though I started out in college as a physics major) that it uses up energy to keep turning lights on and off. After checking with our public power company, Con Edison, I found my mother is absolutely right...this is just another *OWT*! Flipping a switch simply breaks (Off) or completes (On) an electrical circuit, and does not use any energy, electrical, that is. Of course, it still requires human energy to flip the switch.

If that's the problem around your house (and it does take time to break habits). Con Ed points out that at 13.2 cents per kwh, a 100-watt bulb costs 1.3 cents per hour of use. This may not seem like very much, but it sure adds up by the time the bill comes. They also have some tips on saving electricity...and money.

- Keep the bulbs and fixtures clean so you get maximum light from the bulb.
- Light-colored shades are best for releasing the most light.
- Use light colors on walls and ceilings to reflect light.
- Use lower wattage bulbs for halls, vestibules, and other places where you don't need bright lighting.
- Use dimmers to adjust lighting to specific needs. (My favorite place for low lighting is the dining room, but everyone complains they can't see what they're eating.)
- When possible, use one large bulb rather than several smaller ones. One 100-watt incandescent bulb, for example, produces more light than two 60-watt bulbs, with 20 percent less energy consumption.
- Use energy-saving bulbs that have slightly lower wattage than the usual 40, 60, 75, and 100 watts.
- Use an illuminated wall switch instead of a night light.
- Replace incandescent bulbs with the new fluorescent bulbs that screw into any socket. They produce about four times as much light per watt. That means a 40-watt fluorescent bulb is brighter than a 150-watt incandescent bulb. They may cost a little more, but they last twenty times longer and will cut your electric bill.

I really liked the following suggestion for chronic energy wasters: Replace a switch with a spring-wound timer for areas where lights are usually used for short periods, like halls and stairways. It's like a kitchen timer, but instead of a ringing a bell, it cuts off electricity to the light. And it never forgets.

2

Chicken Soup Is the Best Medicine and Other Miracle Cures

Chicken Soup Is the Best Medicine for a Cold. *Maybe*

A sense of great awe comes over me as I approach this old wives' tale. I mean, who am I to comment on one of the universal truths of the ages? But, like the proverbial fool, it is my sworn duty to rush in, even to a place where angels utter not a peep.

I could "chicken" out of this whole challenge by taking refuge behind the one statement about this "Jewish penicillin" that nobody would ever argue with; "It couldn't hurt."

The obvious benefit, when you have read all that is written about treating colds and flu, is that it's the hot liquid characteristic of chicken soup that makes it effective. Colds and fevers tend to dehydrate the body, and cause chills; therefore hot liquids help.

Picky appetites can also be tempted by the aroma and flavor of chicken soup, especially when homemade. Even with the fat skimmed off (current recommendation) it delivers protein, carbohydrates, some vitamins and other helpful nutrients in an easily digested form. This makes it an excellent "first food" during illness.

So far so good.

However, like prunes (see page 56), chicken soup has other qualities, chemical compounds, or whatever you want to call it, that do indeed make it a very effective treatment for colds, flu, and similar ailments.

Where else but in Miami Beach could the scientific principals behind chicken soup be better explored? A study made at the Mt. Sinai Medical Center there found that hot chicken soup, either the smell or the taste, "appears to possess an additional substance for increasing the flow of nasal mucus," this helps removes germs from your system and gets you on the way to recovery.

For those of you who would like to do your own research, here's my mother's recipe. It's delicious even if you aren't sick!

Sadye's Chicken Soup

3- to 4-pound cut-up frying or stewing chicken, including gizzard and heart, but not the liver (I also take off the skin because it's supposed to have chemicals in it.)

1 whole onion
2 large carrots, peeled and sliced
2 stalks celery with leaves, chopped
1 medium or large parsnip, peeled and sliced
2 sprigs chopped fresh parsley, or 2 teaspoons flakes
1/2 teaspoon dry dill weed
1 Tablespoon chicken soup mix granules, or 2 chicken broth cubes

1. Place all ingredients into large pot and cover with 2 quarts cold water.
2. Cover and bring to a boil; then skim off top.
3. Partially cover and simmer for about 2 1/2 to 3 hours.
4. Remove chicken, then pour mixture through strainer.
5. Press carrots and parsnip through strainer (this gives the soup a nice color and flavor)
6. For a richer soup (super strength), cook uncovered for another 15 minutes.
7. Chill, then remove the fat.

If the patient has an appetite, you can add some cooked rice or noodles.

Milk Is Good for an Ulcer.   *Not True*

This one is so entrenched in the media, it's become a cliche...someone at the bar says, with a grimace, "Just gimme a glass of milk." And everyone knows he's nursing an ulcer, is probably anxious, uptight, etc. with just that one line, a writer can convey a complete personality.

Until fairly recently, generations of people suffering the

pain of gastric ulcers were advised, even by doctors, to regularly drink milk as part of the treatment. It seemed to make sense since, after all, milk could be digested by infants and certainly wasn't spicy. However, research has now shown that, instead of soothing an ulcer, milk actually aggravates the condition.

An ulcer occurs in the stomach or duodenum when acid secretion wears away an area of the protective mucous lining. Milk, while it may seem to be a bland food, actually stimulates the production of gastric acid...which only increases the irritation and pain. Other culprits creating excessive acid include stress, smoking, caffeine, alcohol, poor nutrition, lack of sleep and the use of some medications like aspirin.

A bland diet may help relieve the symptoms during an acute attack, but it doesn't heal an ulcer...or prevent one from occurring. The good news...new research at the Baylor College of Medicine in Houston indicates that nearly all ulcers are caused by a common bacteria, *Helicobacter pylori*. In their study, taking a combination of two common antibiotics (to kill the bacteria), an ulcer drug, and over-the-counter medication for an upset stomach did more than just heal the ulcers. Ninety-five percent of patients with gastric ulcers had no recurrence in the next two years. So if you're one of the ten million Americans who suffer from ulcers, check with your doctor.

You Have to Suck the Poison Out of a Snake Bite.   *Not True*

Would I really have the guts to do it? Would you? Well, save your saliva, here is just another old wives' take.. perpetuated by, who else? Hollywood. In Western movies someone is always saving his best friend by making quick cuts around the bite and then sucking out the venom.

Doctors point out that cutting just enlarges the wound, and applying your mouth to the area only increases the risk of bacterial infection. It's actually the worst thing you can do. Tourniquets are also no-no's because they cut off blood supply to the area and the tissue may be damaged. So don't even think about whipping off your belt and looking for a stick. Ice packs can be useful to reduce swelling, but not to the point of causing frostbite.

Luckily, most snakes aren't poisonous, and even those that are may not give lethal bites. For any bite, the best advice is to get medical care as soon as possible. If you're going camping in remote areas where you might encounter poisonous snakes, it's smart to carry an emergency snake bite kit.

Put Butter on a Burn Right Away.   *Not True*

Once again, the wisdom of the ages can be a dangerous thing. Rubbing butter, oil, or ointment immediately on a burn only helps to keep the heat in and increases the damage to tissue and blood vessels. Later on, for a minor burn, it's fine to use bacitracin ointment, juice from an aloe vera leaf, or vitamin E oil.

The first thing you should do is to cool the area. Remember, even if the skin looks only a little red, burns are usually worse than they first appear because the heat is still penetrating below the surface of the skin.

Here's what the experts say to do immediately for scalds and flame burns.

1. If the burned area is covered with clothing, first pour cool water on the burn, then remove the soaked or scorched clothing, unless it's stuck to the skin.
2. Immerse the area in cool water or apply cool wet

compresses for ten to fifteen minutes. If the compresses get warm, pour cold water over them. Never put ice directly on the skin because it can cause further damage.

3. If the injured area is larger than a half-inch, or the burn has destroyed the skin, call your doctor.

4. In cases of extensive burns, after cooling the areas, wrap the victim in a clean sheet, then a blanket to prevent losing body heat. Get help or go to an emergency room at once.

A few weeks ago, a friend sadly told me that his 15-month-old grandson was severely scalded after tipping a cup of hot tea all over himself. Since they lived across the street from the hospital, they picked him up and rushed him over to the emergency room...a natural reaction. But even during that short time, the burning continued. I thought..if only they had immediately poured on cool water, stripped off his clothing, put him in a cool bath for a few minutes, and then gone to the hospital. Of course, this wasn't the time to say anything.

Feed a Cold, Starve a Fever. *Not True*

Here's another *OWT* that is so ingrained that we don't even question it. But there's one problem, a problem that surfaced again as we asked a doctor for some medical backup.

The doctor began talking about feeding colds and starving fevers when he suddenly stopped, scratched his head and said, "Or is it 'Feed a fever and starve a cold'?"

Anyway, he went on to say it really doesn't matter, since neither one is true. If you need one simple answer to this it should probably be "drown 'em both." Because both colds and fevers are helped by liquids. Fever can be caused by a variety of things. Whatever its cause, it is a condition that dehydrates the body, and therefore fluids should usually be ingested.

In addition, the advice is that when a person has a cold, and is hungry, by all means he or she should eat. If you go along with most of the medical community, which now acknowledges some benefit from vitamin C, then you should especially eat and drink those fruits and vegetables that are high in vitamin C. Your body can also use the energy supplied by a well-balanced diet.

So the dictum should actually be changed to...Feed a Cold, Feed a Fever!

Use an Alcohol Rub to Lower a Fever.   *Not True*

Even though I may be done with the torture of getting through countless finals and regents' exams, miscellaneous flotsam and jetsam of knowledge pop to the surface of my mind every now and then, usually it is triggered by a subliminal stimulus. This is such a moment.

Thinking about alcohol rubs, I suddenly remember that "evaporation is a cooling process." If you share my childhood memories of being sponged periodically when sick, with that accompanying terrible smell, then it all seems to make sense. Alcohol evaporates very quickly when sponged on the skin and therefore cools the skin quickly, if only temporarily. So this is one practice that should be right on the money.

As recently as ten years ago, doctors routinely recommended the use of alcohol sponge baths, especially in the armpits and between the legs, as a means of lowering temperature. Now this advice has been reduced to the status of just another old wives' tale. It's true that an alcohol sponge bath might reduce a fever, but the alcohol can be absorbed through the skin, and the fumes are dangerous to breathe, something I must have instinctively suspected as a child because I remember trying to hold my breath.

The American Academy of Pediatrics (AAP) now warns against giving alcohol sponge baths to infants and children. Instead, doctors recommend a lukewarm tub or sponge bath to lower a temperature, since water also evaporates and has a cooling action.

By the way, another recent change in medical thinking concerns the use of aspirin to lower a child's fever. In cases of viral illnesses like flu, colds, or chicken pox, the AAP warns against giving aspirin to children under age sixteen. Why? Aspirin has been associated with the development of Reye's syndrome, a potentially life-threatening condition. However, it's all right to give acetaminophen or ibuprofen.

But wait a minute, you're probably thinking, "Let's get back to the bath!" What about this golden rule...

Never Take a Bath When You're Sick. *Not True*

Tell this one to my husband and you'll get an argument—and one of his famous war stories. Not a war story, actually it's more of a basic training story.

Having grown up "sweating" out fevers—more than likely with sulfa powders—my husband had always believed that washing one's fevered frame with anything but alcohol meant instant death. So, when he found himself ill and feverish one night while he was in the Army, he made sure to work up a good sweat and slept in a soaking wet tent with soaking wet clothing (to be discussed in another OWT). When he was sent to the post hospital, the army doctors immediately tossed him into a shower. With his initial shock worn off, and tucked snugly between clean sheets, he realized that, not only he didn't die, but it was a lot more pleasant to be sick and clean than sick and smelly.

Since then, whenever he comes down with a flu or a bad

cold, he may not always be the best patient, but he's definitely the cleanest, taking at least a couple of showers a day, especially when he has chills and fever.

It works for my husband, but what do doctors say? The answer is that baths and even shampoos are perfectly fine, for children as well as adults. Not only does it make you feel better, but as you've read, it also helps lower a fever. Just be sure to dry off in a warm room.

Soothe an Earache With a Few Drops of Warm Oil.   *Not true*

Ear infections are common among young children because their eustachian tubes, which go from the middle ear to the back of the throat, are shorter and narrower. This makes it easier for germs to travel to the middle ear and cause infection. When the eustachian tube swells or closes, the fluid builds up, creating severe pain. Even an adult with an earache is often in desperate need of relief.

But warm oil is not the answer. Most doctors warn this treatment is at best useless and could be dangerous if the eardrum is perforated. One recent home medical book does suggest using a few drops of warm oil, but only "if there is no drainage" or "liquid in the ear." However, why take a chance of making the wrong judgment when there's nothing to be gained. Pediatrician Dr. Jeffrey L. Brown also notes, "Although parents may be tempted to give their child a decongestant-antihistamine preparation to help drain and dry up the fluid, studies suggest that they can actually make the condition worse."

Instead, doctors recommend using a painkiller like aspirin (or an aspirin substitute for children); elevating the head to help relieve pressure on the ear; and applying warmth to the outside of the ear. Then get to the doctor, because most middle ear infections respond best to antibiotics. Left untreated, they may cause burst eardrums and loss of hearing.

You Can Cure Hiccups By: *Maybe*

—Swallowing a Teaspoon of Sugar.
—Blowing Into a Paper Bag.
—Being Surprised.
—Holding Your Breath For One Minute.

We don't know how prehistoric man handled his hiccups, but there's no question he had them, people have been hiccuping since the dawn of creation. Now, through the wonders of ultrasound, we can even see the fetus hiccup inside the uterus. After all those years, one would think that doctors could have identified the cause and the cure.

Think again.

Hiccups remain a medical mystery. Experts believe that hiccups start when something disrupts the rhythmic movement of the diaphragm, a dome-shaped muscle that stretches between the lungs and the stomach. It contracts and pulls air into the lungs when you inhale, and pushes air into the lungs when you inhale, then relaxes and pushes air back out when you exhale. The most likely explanations given for the disruption are eating too much, which causes the enlarged stomach to press on the diaphragm, and taking in too much air, which thus disrupts regular breathing.

All this sounds reasonable as to how hiccups start, but what about stopping them? Over the centuries, there have been thousands of cures, in addition to the ones above, that people swear by. The *Journal of Clinical Gastroenterology* has even published the following list of suggestions:

- Yank forcefully on the tongue.
- Lift the uvula (that little flap at the back of your mouth) with a spoon (trying not to gag!).
- Chew and swallow dry bread.
- Suck a lemon wedge soaked with Angostura bitters. (Yuck!)
- Compress the chest by pulling the knees up or leaning forward.
- Gargle with water.
- Hold your breath for one minute.

The general idea is to overwhelm the nerve impulses that cause the hiccuping (maybe that's why being surprised might help), or to increase the carbon dioxide levels in the blood (the logic behind blowing into a paper bag.) My favorite remedy—drinking water from the opposite side of a glass—doesn't seem to fit either category. However, as one doctor has pointed out, "Anytime you have lots of ways to treat something it means that none of them works very well; otherwise, there would be only one way to treat it."

The bottom line is that whatever works for you, by all means use it. Fortunately, most hiccups will stop on their own within a few minutes, even if you ignore them. But then there's poor Charles Osborne (1894—1990). He led a normal life, married twice and fathered eight children. His main problem was keeping his false teeth in place. He holds the Guiness World record for hiccups 69 years, until his death.

Never Squeeze a Boil.   *True*

I sometimes wonder if, in the annals of psychotic behavior, there isn't a big fat file on people who like to squeeze boils. We've all met them. Upon sighting a boil a strange glaze crosses their eyes, their forefingers extend into a pincerlike shape and they advance upon the boil like predatory beasts.

It's important to be able to impart the latest medical advice: the best way to handle a boil is to apply a warm compress and wait for it to "come to a head." Less satisfying and more time-consuming it may be, but it lessens the chance of the various complications squeezing can engender.

But first, what exactly is a boil?

A boil is formed when bacteria, called staphyloccus, gets into the skin and infects a blocked oil gland or hair follicle. This triggers a defense reaction in the body and white blood cells are rallied to the area. The ensuing conflagration produces pus which raises the skin in a red, angry boil. And therein lies the danger of squeezing.

If the boil has not come to a head (a white or yellowish

area at the peak of the swelling), squeezing can force the bacteria into the bloodstream, and possibly into the lymph system. If the infection travels to the brain, or if the person is nursing or diabetic, it can be very dangerous. Fever, chills, or swellings of lymph nodes are signs that this spreading has occurred.

Warm compresses applied every few hours will bring the boil to a head in a few days. Or the body may simply reabsorb it. Once a small boil comes to a head, and there is no sign of spreading infection, it is okay to lance it with a sterilized needle. Once the boil is draining, it's best to keep up the warm compresses and keep the area clean.

The Best Way to Stop a Nosebleed Is to: *Not true*

—Put a Wad of Paper Under Your Lip.
—Put Ice on the Back of Your Neck.
—Tip Your Head Back.

My husband, who played football in the days before face protectors and is therefore very familiar with bloody noses, swears by the wad of cloth or paper under the lip...he was back in the game within seconds. Besides sports injuries, nosebleeds can be caused by minor things such as picking, blowing your nose too hard, (or too often), excessive sneezing or coughing, and, in some cases, very dry air.

Dr. Henry Heimlich (of "maneuver" fame) says that most of these minor bleeding episodes will stop shortly, even if left alone. He also advises, in *Dr. Heimlich's Guide to Emergency Medical Situations*, first applying pressure at the bleeding site by pressing the outside of the nostril toward the middle of the nose against the bony cartilage there. This pressure should be maintained for at least three minutes or longer, until the blood clots. That means no peeking to see if it has stopped.

Ice packs, or cold compresses, are advisable if the bleeding doesn't stop, but Dr. Heimlich says to put the compress or pack on the face, above the nose or right on the bridge of the nose, not at the back of the neck.

Tilting the head back is another OWT without basis. This makes the blood run down the throat and into the lungs only hiding the fact that the flow is continuing. The victim should actually be kept sitting upright, with the head in a normal position so the blood flows out of the nose instead of down the throat.

If the flow does not abate, and especially if it is bright red and profuse—which could indicate arterial bleeding— keep the pressure on and rush the victim to a medical emergency facility or doctor. If nose bleeds are persistent or recurring, especially in the very young and the older adult, a doctor should be consulted.

Does the wad of paper work? It's supposed to apply pressure to the blood vessels in the nose, so that flow stops and the blood can clot. But pinching the nose with two fingers is really more effective. However, my husband points out the former was more practical. After all, in those days a bloody nose wasn't enough to keep a player out of the game, and the wad under the lip kept the hands free to play football. Did it really stop the bleeding? Who knew? Who cared? The important thing was, who won?

Put Mud on a Boil.   *True*

Now, what about using mud, preferably from a wasp's nest? This is just one of a whole slew of OWTs about the treatment of boils. According to The *Doctors Book of Home Remedies*, people also swear by things like poultices of warm milk and bread, burdock leaves, a heated slice of tomato, a raw onion, mashed garlic, and tea. Denver mud is available over the counter in some pharmacies and is

36

certainly easier, and safer, to obtain than wasp's mud. This arsenal of anti-boil weapons may be as effective as the warm compresses in bringing the boil to a head. There really isn't any research to confirm one way or another.

However, once the boil begins to drain, if the bacteria in all these remedies get into the bloodstream, that can be as dangerous as the boil bacteria. So make sure and use the mud, before the boil begins to drain!

Put a Steak on a Black Eye.   *True*

Remember how in cartoons and comic books—poor Jiggs as Maggie went after him with her trusty rolling pin—they always showed the character, a split second after receiving a punch, with a large fresh steak on his eye? This habit more than likely got its start when steak was twenty five cents a pound. But then again, nobody says you can't rub a steak with barbecue sauce and broil it after it's been used on a shiner.

My husband vividly remembers that his first black eye came at the hands of a kid named Wilfred who left him with a steak on his eye, and a constant reminder from his mother about how much it cost.

We asked Dr. John Seeder, an ophthalmologist practicing in New York city (where black eyes are not at all uncommon) for advice. He pointed out that a black eye was simply a bruise, just like a black-and-blue mark, with all the attendant broken blood vessels and swelling. The best treatment for a bruise is an immediate application of anything cold, preferably something with a bit of flexibility that can conform to the contours of the face. Cold works in two ways: It keeps the swelling down, and it helps stop the internal bleeding (the source of that mottled coloring) by constricting the broken blood vessels.

Think about it. In 1950, what could you count on to be

cold, flexible, and immediately available? Right! A piece of meat from the fridge. Cold compresses were too slow (remember those plastic sleeves filled with ice cubes? Ugh!), and rags soaked with cold water held their temperature for about two minutes—unless you got your shiner in the wintertime. Plus, the curved ends of a steak fit so comfortably over the abused socket!

A couple of things doctors advise not to do: don't take aspirin or blow your nose. Aspirin acts as an anticoagulant and slows the blood clotting. And, if the blow was pretty severe, there could be minor fractures of the eye socket. Blowing one's nose is another no-no. It can force air into the area and cause increased swelling.

Bedrest Is Best for Backache.   *Not True*

Almost everyone is familiar with backaches. The American Academy of Orthopedic Surgeons rates back pain second to the common cold for causing employee absenteeism. According to most studies, four out of five people suffer a form of this affliction at some point in their lives.

Our pain began—when else?—with prehistoric man. Always eager to move things along, evolution built-in the problem when it straightened man up from walking on all fours to walking upright on his hind legs. Without the spine changing in some structural way to support the upright position, man didn't have a chance of a happy life walking on two feet. It's cold comfort to know we all start out with the same slight handicap.

The universal prescription for an aching back has always been bedrest, sometimes supplemented by traction devices and strong muscle-relaxing medications. Staying horizontal seems to makes sense and usually helps relieve the pain...until you stand up. So begins the cycle of chronic pain.

Recently, however, doctors have discovered that bedrest may actually be harmful. With prolonged bedrest there is a significant loss of muscle strength and tone as well as loss of calcium from the bones. Even if you're in pain, inactivity can be more harmful than exercise. One reconditioning program which offers special workouts was developed by researchers at the University of Texas Southwest Medical Center in Dallas. Their program permanently returns nearly nine out of ten workers with back injuries to their jobs. That's more than twice the results produced by traditional treatments of prolonged rest.

Instead of popping painkillers and taking to bed, ask your doctor about a comprehensive program of physical exercises, muscle strengthening, and stress reduction.

Rub Snow on Frostbite. *Not True*

If, like me, you were brought up in cold winter climes, your first acquaintance with frostbite most likely came as a child. My family moved to upstate New York from Pennsylvania when I was a little girl; my mother wasn't really aware of the extreme difference in temperature in those two places. One cold but sunny morning she let me go out to play the same way I had in Harrisburg, PA. A horrified neighbor called to ask if my mother realized that it was ten below zero—with a monster windchill factor—which could cause almost instant frostbite. I was back in the house within seconds.

It was then that I first heard the OWT about rubbing snow on frostbite: that's exactly what the neighbor advised my mother to do to treat the little white spots that had begun to form on my face. I survived without permanent damage, but it's always struck me as a little strange...like treating a burn with fire.

Not only is it strange, but it's actually dangerous. Water conducts cold more quickly than air, and since snow and ice are crystallized forms of water, they aggravate the freezing of the skin. Rubbing the frozen tissue does not increase circulation, it only further damages the skin and underlying tissue. The logic behind the persistent claims for this OWT's veracity eludes most experts.

Frostbite can be an extremely serious condition, one that can easily result in irreversible tissue damage. It must be treated properly.

It is also a very sneaky condition. Unlike most injuries which are usually accompanied by pain, frostbite begins with numbness, leaving its victims, especially children, unaware that anything is happening to them. The beginning stage (what I probably had) is called frostnip and affects the cheeks, nose, ears, and uncovered fingers. White spots and numbness, the first indications, are signals that you should get out of the cold as quickly as possible. If that's not possible, get out of the wind.

Warming the affected parts comes next. Skiers quickly learn that the best way to warm up is to use your own body. If it's the face that is affected, place your hands on the spot and warm it with your fingers. You can also cup your hands over your face and blow warm air onto the skin surface. If it is your fingertips that are affected, get them under your armpits or, better yet, eschew decorum and stick them inside your pants.

The American Academy of Pediatrics also recommends gradually warming the frostbitten skin with warm (not hot) water or compresses as soon as possible. But don't rub the area. The skin is very fragile. When thawed, the frostbitten area may turn blue or purple, or it may swell and blister. The pain that accompanies thawing may have been the source of the idea that rubbing ice on the affected area was preferable to warmth. The ice increases freezing and numbness, producing less pain.

The best cure, of course, is to be aware of the dangers of extreme cold and windchill. And remember, if your clothes or shoes are wet, the temperature doesn't even have to drop below freezing for frostbite to set in.

Cases of severe frostbite require a visit to the emergency room or doctor.

Knock on the Head? Stay Awake to Prevent a Concussion. *Not True*

In grade school, I was swung headfirst into the iron post of a "maypole"...no wonder they've disappeared from modern playgrounds. After the crash I started walking home, began to feel very dizzy, and passed out with my first concussion. Had someone been around to get me up right away, could the concussion have been prevented? Not really.

Jeffrey Brown, M.D., writes, "Some parents mistakenly believe that keeping the child awake after a head injury will prevent a concussion." If a child has been crying and is exhausted, many pediatricians say it's all right to allow him to sleep for up to half an hour. The purpose of waking him up is to make sure he is arousable. If the injury occurs at night, the recommendation is to wake him up at least twice. But when there's a sudden loss of consciousness, like I had, it's important to get the doctor immediately. This holds true for adults as well as children.

Upset Tummy? Eat Crackers, Drink Flat Ginger Ale or Coke, Eat Ginger. *True*

Not too long ago, one of the hazards of world travel was the inevitable malaise, the one that kept you on a short leash to *la toilette*. Call it the water, the fatigue, the difference in time, the unfamiliar foods, for some a touch of motion sickness, and just the overdoing of everything. Whatever the problem, you usually get an earful of advice in the form of local OWTs from hotel managers, chambermaids, and assorted fellow travelers.

Sometimes such advice actually proves helpful and you can discover local remedies that may work wonders. In France, the best one I learned of was an aperitif called Fernet Branca. It was the one of the most bitter, worst-tasting fluids I have ever tasted—but it's nothing short of a miracle.

In America we have our own set of OWT cures that we can recommend to queasy foreigners: the most familiar being ginger ale or Coca-Cola, drunk after they have gone flat. We also have heard that eating dry crackers, like soda crackers, is also an effective ploy. But do they really work?

Before continuing with the answer, let's first explore the differences in the kinds of upset stomach. Some upset stomachs appear around Thanksgiving and Christmas, the kind we get from food and alcohol overindulgence. But another common cause, experienced particularly by travelers, is motion sickness—mal de mer—which can happen on land and in the air as well as at sea. This is caused by a whole series of confusing messages from the brain to the stomach and can interfere with the normal actions of the digestive system. These messages may be triggered by the eyes, the ears, or the brain in a variety of scenarios that we won't get into here.

Although the triggering action for upset stomachs may differ between those caused by overindulgence and those caused by brain messages, the effect is similar: acids form, causing nausea and vomiting.

The question, then, is can we turn to OWTs for, if not a cure, then some relief?

Ginger really is a proven remedy for motion sickness. Made from a root, this spice has been used for centuries by ocean travelers, and recently passed muster in a series of scientific evaluations. In one test it was found that two powdered gingerroot capsules were more effective than an over-the-counter medication in preventing motion sickness.

According to the people at the Travelers Health care Center at the University Hospitals of Cleveland, ginger works for stomach upset by absorbing acids in the gastrointestinal tract and thereby reducing nausea. Some sailing friends swear by fresh ginger, but others say it causes indigestion and heartburn. We can't tell you how much ginger is contained in the various ginger ales on the market, but it seems to help minor upsets: the liquid is also of value for the dehydration that usually accompanies stomach upset and vomiting. You drink it flat because the gas from carbonation is undesirable for an upset stomach.

Although the Coca-Cola base syrup is supposed to be a well-guarded secret, it is probably based on a common stomach remedy of the last century. A very close relative of this formula, called Unterberg, is known to German-Americans, who buy it in their ethnic delicatessens. Like Fernet Branca this pretty foul-tasting syrup has been a dependable stomach remedy for many years.

These cola syrups are effective in most cases after the sickness has begun. They don't cure it, but they do provide some relief. The recommendation about drinking ginger ale flat also goes for coke, although some people find that the burping action from the carbonation offers some relief from nausea.

Plain soda crackers—another common remedy—have two pluses. First, they are easily digestible and bland, and can absorb some of the offending fluids in your stomach. Second, they contain bicarbonate of soda and cream of tartar, which help neutralize acids. They're also easy to carry around. We always keep some on our sailboat.

Just in passing...much of the research material we have read on this subject says that motion sickness comes on rapidly. Our experience with sailing guests indicates there are some forewarnings to seasickness: One of these is yawning, followed by drowsiness. If the drowsy person is fed some Coca-Cola and crackers, or a ginger capsule at this stage—combined with heading for calmer waters—they may escape having mal de mer. Avoiding an upset stomach, on other occasions, usually requires sidestepping that extra helping.

Copper Bracelets Relieve Arthritis.　　*Maybe*

The only well-preserved spine of the Neanderthal man showed signs of arthritis; the use of copper to combat arthritis goes back at least as far as ancient Egypt. However, in researching the truth of this timeless claim, I found expert after expert dismissing the copper bracelet as quackery or a placebo. So how, given the lack of substantiation, has this OWT lasted for so long?

We found very interesting facts about copper in a book published in 1989 by Dr. Felix Fernandez-Madrid, a noted rheumatologist. The approach taken by Dr. Fernandez-Madrid seemed an enlightened one, taking into consideration—in addition to physical conditions—the particular role of psychological factors in cases of rheumatoid arthritis. He suggests that even a quack therapist can positively affect the arthritis sufferer by the mere suggestion of relief.

Dr. Fernandez-Madrid states that much of how sufferers feel has to do with how they think about their pain and stiffness. If the inevitable green stain from a copper bracelet does nothing else, it certainly *looks* as if it is working. Studies show that about one-third of those taking a placebo do improve, although it usually lasts only a brief time. Scientists believe that, with all placebos, the body releases chemicals which promote a positive effect.

In 1981 and 1982, Dr. W. R. Walker and his associates did a clinical trial and follow-up on the effect that wearing a copper bracelet could have on inflammatory diseases. The tests showed that copper dissolves in sweat and can leach in through the skin. In fact, most of the copper bracelets actually lost part of their mass to this process and microscopic particles of copper penetrated the skins of cats, pigs, bulls, and even human beings.

Those who wore the copper bracelets reported improvement, while those who did not reported no improvement at all. Attempts to use placebo bracelets in some tests were negated by the fact the real copper causes the greening of the immediate skin area. Basically, nothing much was determined by these tests other than establishing the "possibility" there is some benefit. However, as Dr. Fernandez-Madrid says... there is still a lot of research to be done.

More recently, Helmar Dollwet, Ph.D. of the University of Akron, theorized that some cases of arthritis might be caused by individual differences in the ability to metabolize normal copper requirements from food. Those who cannot absorb sufficient supplies may be able to get their copper from the bracelet. But this, too, awaits more research and confirmation. For now, "stay tuned" for new developments. There is still much interest in the anti-inflammatory effects of certain metals and so we should be seeing some interesting new findings. So far as the curative powers of copper, the Arthritis Foundation advises, "There is no scientific evidence that copper bracelets have any benefit for arthritis." The only reported adverse effect is the reaction between copper and perspiration to produce a blue-green stain on the skin.

Among other unproven, but harmless, remedies for arthritis are acupuncture, mineral springs, spas, topical creams, vibrators, and vinegar and honey. The latter was given testimonial by a friend of my mother's who has reached her eighties without a twinge of arthritis. She attributes this to having taken one teaspoon of vinegar, mixed with one teaspoon of honey, in a cup of hot water every day since she was in her twenties.

A recent television news show reported new research which indicates that a daily serving of 2 grapefruits, or 2 oranges, or one-half head of broccoli can be as effective as taking one commonly prescribed anti-inflammatory pill. If true, these foods could offer additional benefits without the possible stomach irritation that can result from medication.

Fish oil has also gained some measure of scientific support as a treatment for arthritis. In research at the Albany Medical Center, findings indicate that, taken as a highly refined supplement, fish oil can help suppress the symptoms of rheumatoid arthritis, an auto immune disease.

The Arthritis Foundation is the best source of reliable information about treatments, effective or unproven, safe or harmful. (Their toll-free hotline is 800-283-7800.)

To Get Rid of Whooping Cough, Get Out on the Water.   *Not True*

The trauma of a whooping cough treatment left my mother afraid to swim or ride a boat. Some old wives' tales can be hazardous to your mental health.

When she was a young child, my mother and her four sisters all came down with the illness, and were all coughing, at the same time. Her desperate mother was advised by a neighbor to "take them out on a body of water." So her father dutifully loaded the girls into a small boat and rowed them to the middle of a little pond in a nearby park. My mother vividly remembers the boat rocking until, of course, it tipped over. Luckily, the pond was very shallow and no one was hurt. Whether it was the result of being on the water or the shock of going in, she swears that every-one's whooping cough was cured.

Since breathing moist air—is generally advised for coughing, the old wives' tale wisdom which suggests getting to water has an instinctive correctness—as many OWTs do. Pediatricians recommend using a vaporizer, or sitting in a steam-filled bathroom, to relieve coughing or croup. Whooping cough (pertussis), however, is a serious respiratory disease which can cause brain damage and even death. It requires a trip to the doctor, not the lake. More importantly, protect children through proper immunization with the DTP vaccine.

Saunas Are the Best Way to Clean Skin. *Not True*

Scandinavians have been sweating in saunas for centuries. The Romans liked the heat too, building steam baths everywhere they went.

These days, nearly every health club and gym has some version of a sauna and/or steam room; the sales of items like home saunas and facial "steamers" have skyrocketed. There's no doubt that people are sweating in record numbers, so it must have some benefit. Doctors agree that the heat does help relieve muscle tension and can make you feel more relaxed. But is all that sweating a path to true cleanliness?

Not according to the University of California's *Berkeley Wellness Letter*. In answer to a reader's question, "Do saunas really cleanse the skin?", they point out, "The sauna's heat does enhance blood flow near the skin's surface and may thereby give you a 'healthy glow,' but the sweating won't cleanse the body of bacteria any more effectively than a warm shower. In fact, a shower with soap will cleanse the skin better." They also warn that a sauna may actually aggravate certain skin conditions, such as dry skin, acne, or dermatitis.

You Can Sweat Out a Cold. *Not True*

And what about the notion that heavy sweating and opening up your pores to get rid of all kinds of toxins will actually "sweat out a cold?" The answer, once again from the esteemed doctors on the editorial board of the University of California's *Berkeley Wellness Letter*, is conveyed in just one word—"nonsense!"

Dealing With Bees, Wasps and hornets

Is it the actual pain or the surprise of being stung by these tiny flying creatures that so fills us with terror as we try to relax in the summer sun? Centuries of old wives have been buzzing with advice on avoiding them, dealing with them, and treating their painful bites. Here are some of the most commonly heard tales.

Don't Wear Bright Colors, Especially Red, Because They Attract Bees. *Maybe*

Talk to five entomologists and you'll get five different opinions on how well bees can distinguish bright colors.

A few years ago I did a TV segment on bee stings, and the ABC Standards and Practices office required three expert sources to back up each statement. After consulting with at least ten authorities from all parts of the country, and learning more than I ever wanted to know about bee-vision, the only agreement I found was this...

- Patterns—even black and white patterns—are more likely to attract the interest of a bee than any color.
- The safest colors are simply solid white and tan.

Everyone concurred that a bee's sense of smell is sharper

than his eyesight. It's the sweet smell of flowers that draws his attention. So if you're going gardening, hiking or on a picnic, don't use scented soaps, suntan lotions, hair spray, and—obviously—no perfume! Other protective measures include: always wearing shoes because bees get a bit riled when stepped on; don't even think about poking into holes or woodpiles that might contain nests; and checking open juice and soda cans before drinking. I don't even want to think about the possibility of swallowing a bee!

If You Don't Move, You Won't Get Stung. *Not True*

Your will power is stronger than mine if you can stand still when you're being attacked by a swarm of bees, wasps, or hornets. It did actually flash through my mind when, many years ago, I was walking with my young daughter near the woods and encountered a group of very angry yellow jackets that had been routed out by a small brush fire. Instead, I picked her up and ran for my life.

Bee experts say if you do overcome your fear and stand still, your reward will most likely be multiple stings. They agree it's best to follow the natural instinct for self-preservation and surpass your personal best in the 100-yard dash. Also, if you've ever had a secret urge to careen around a corner or tear madly through the brush, this would be a good excuse to indulge yourself, just so you can lose the swarm.

But, if it's just one or two insects who've been attracted by some food or perfume, don't panic and start swatting. The movement can attract them, and one might sting out of self-defense if you happen to make contact. Just keep cool and they'll go about their business.

If You Get Stung, Put Some Mud on the Spot   *True*

Once again, there's wisdom in a wives' tale—even if you have to dig for it. Since mud is likely to be cool it can help relieve the pain and swelling of a sting. Ice—or anything cold, like a soda can—is much more effective and less likely to cause infection than mud. An oral antihistamine and pain reliever may also be helpful. My daughter and I did get several stings, and I remember that sitting in a cool baking soda bath helped a lot.

Doctors also advise that if the offending stinger from a wasp or bee is still in the skin, it should be removed before applying any treatment. But don't just pluck it out, because in the process you may squeeze the venom sac and make matters worse. Instead, gently scrape the stinger out with something like a credit card or your fingernail. In the case of a honeybee, don't try to remove the stinger because it has a barb that will stick in the skin. Left alone, it will dissolve in a few days.

A small percentage of people experience a much more severe and generalized allergic reaction to insect stings. The symptoms can include dizziness, fever, difficulty breathing, and muscle pains. Since this could be life-threatening, it's important to get medical help as soon as possible.

If You Get Stung Once, the Next Time Will Be Worse. *Not True*

Some doctors feel that, as with other allergens, repeated bee stings can increase hypersensitivity to the point of potentially fatal reactions. However, recent research has disproved this theory.

One study made at Johns Hopkins University also showed that out of 174 children who did have a previous serious reaction, only 9% had another serious reaction when stung at a later time. For the others, the reactions was less severe. Although chances can be reduced by taking an allergy shot, most children seem to outgrow their sensitivity.

All this may be reassuring, but I know it won't help very much the next time a persistent bee starts zeroing in.

Wearing a Clove of Garlic Around Your Neck Keeps You From Getting Sick. *Not True*

During the devastating Spanish flu epidemic of 1918, my mother recalls that she, along with her four siblings and parents, always wore fresh cloves of garlic, tucked in little bags, on a string around her neck. These peculiar necklaces (other people recall wearing camphor instead of garlic) have been thought—from as far back as the Middle Ages—to provide protection against catching coughs and colds.

It's true that the entire family did stay healthy, but the most likely explanation is that no one came near enough to spread the flu germ. Fortunately for me, my mother did not believe strongly enough to perpetuate this particular old wives' tale during my school years.

Although wearing garlic may not have any practical value, eating garlic has been proven to be very beneficial...especially for the circulatory system. In controlled studies, large doses of garlic, given to healthy subjects for six months, significantly lowered blood cholesterol and triglyceride levels, and also raised the high-density lipoproteins (HDLs). The results became even more impressive when patients with heart disease and elevated cholesterol levels ate the equivalent of one ounce of raw garlic a day. Garlic has been shown to help lower blood pressure in some people.

Less well documented is the effectiveness of eating raw garlic to ward off colds and sore throats. But many people swear that it really works.

If you want to avoid the pitfalls of consuming raw garlic, but still reap the benefits, why not try microwaving an entire head. Just put it into a cup with a little liquid and 1 tablespoon of oil, cover tightly, cook for five minutes and let it stand for five minutes. It's easy and delicious!

Taking Large Amounts of Vitamin C Can Prevent Colds.   *Maybe*

The controversy on this one has been raging ever since Nobel scientist Dr. Linus Pauling published research on vitamin C back in the 1970s. Various studies have either refuted or supported its usefulness, and entire books have been written on the subject. The latest medical thinking seems to be that it may work for some people to reduce the severity of symptoms.

For me, the bottom line is that, like chicken soup, it doesn't hurt, and may actually help. From personal experience, my husband and I have found that taking 1,500 mg. of vitamin C every few hours, when we first feel symptoms coming on, often does stop a cold in its tracks. But not always!

Another Vitamin C note: In a recent study published in the prestigious journal, *Proceedings of the National Academy of Science*, a direct relationship was shown between a diet low in vitamin C and an increased DNA damage in sperm cells. According to one of the researchers, one implication is that increased vitamin C intake could prevent the damage to DNA because of oxidation, the consequences of which include infertility and decreased sperm function in the father, and some mutations, birth defects, and cancers in the offspring.

The recommended daily intake of vitamin C is 250 mg., about the equivalent of seven servings of fruits and vegetables. Since smoking also reduces a person's level of vitamin C, the advice is to either stop smoking, eat more fruits and vegetables, or take a daily supplement.

Tonsils and Adenoids Cause Infections and Should Be Removed. *Not True*

Although I was only eight, I still clearly remember going into the hospital to have my tonsils and adenoids removed: the sweet sick smell of ether, counting backwards until I went under, then waking up with a sharp pain in my throat. The up side was that I was allowed to eat all the ice cream I wanted. Sound familiar? This rather unpleasant experience was shared by most children as a result of the common belief, an "old doctor's tale" that tonsils were the source of infections, especially if they were enlarged. Since children are likely to get frequent sore throats, it's worth sharing the latest medical thinking on the subject.

First of all, instead of causing infections, tonsils are there to help prevent infections from spreading. The purpose of these two masses of tissue at the back of the throat is to "filter" germs from the throat. When bacteria or viruses occasionally infect this filter, the result is tonsillitis. Tonsils and adenoids also contain special cells that produce antibodies to help fight the bacteria and viruses.

As for their size, it's normal for tonsils to be enlarged in early childhood, and then begin to decrease at about six years old. Just because they're big, doesn't mean they have to come out. Adenoids serve much the same function as tonsils, but are less likely to become infected. However, they were often removed at the same time on the theory that "as long as we're operating, why not?"

When is surgery recommended? The American Academy of Pediatrics gives only these five reasons:

1. history of abscesses
2. four or more episodes of tonsillitis in the past year
3. enlarged adenoids producing mouth-breathing
4. hearing loss documented by audiogram
5. hypertension of the pulmonary artery

So there's your answer to anxious, well-meaning grandparents.

Sore Throat Cures

While we're on the subject of sore throats, let's take a look at some of the more common remedies.

Wrap a Scarf Around Your Neck.   *Not True*

Okay, it may not be so common here, but it's an old standby in Europe. Several years ago, we had a very sophisticated French girl visiting us for the summer. One day, she appeared for breakfast with a scarf wrapped several times around her neck. Since it was already 85 degrees F., I asked the natural question, "Why are you wearing a scarf?" Alex replied with obvious disdain for my ignorance, "I have a little sore throat, of course." Needless to say, this measure did very little to help her throat, but by the end of the day, she did have a serious case of prickly heat all over her neck.

An Irish friend uses a scarf as a preventive measure whenever the temperature drops below 60 degrees F., and she swears that whenever she does get a sore throat, it's because she forgot her scarf. I've shown her medical books stating clearly that sore throats are caused by viral infections, strep bacteria, irritation, even post nasal drip, but she'll never be convinced.

Drink Warm Milk With Honey and Whisky.   *Not True*

Of course, I shouldn't laugh at the scarf believers. When I was just out of college, I tried this remedy one night for a scratchy throat. The combination of Scotch, honey, and milk was certainly soothing, but I may have gotten the proportions wrong because I woke up the next morning with a very sore throat...and a bad hangover. A Yugoslavian friend assured me this is a traditional remedy in his country, insisting it should have been Vodka instead of Scotch.

Honey, though, has been revered for thousands of years as an all-purpose cure. The Koran calls it "medicine for man." Hippocrates, the father of modern medicine, praised honey: "It causes heat, cleans sores and ulcers, softens hard ulcers of the lips, heals carbuncles and running sores." The Egyptians, Hindus, Chinese, tribal Africans, and medieval Europeans were just a few of the many other civilizations who used honey both inside and outside the body to treat various ailments.

It seems logical that the sugar in honey may be useful in relieving throat irritation. It certainly doesn't hurt to try. Since most sore throats are caused by viruses, and don't respond to antibiotics, the best bet is to treat the symptoms so the patient feels more comfortable.

Entire books have been devoted to folk remedies containing honey. Is there any scientific basis?

I haven't found any studies specifically made to determine the effectiveness of honey for sore throats. However, research has shown that sugar, the main ingredient in honey, is an antibacterial agent which can help prevent infections and speed healing (although antibiotic ointments are more effective.) So there does seem to be some truth to the old advice to put sugar on a cut!

Recent research conducted in two Maryland hospitals seems to indicate that sugar may also have some analgesic effect. Newborns who were given a small amount of sugar water before having blood drawn or undergoing circumcision, cried less often or for shorter times than those given plain water.

Gargle With Warm Salt Water or Aspirin.   *True*

I was glad to learn this isn't just an OWT. Doctors often advise gargling every few hours with warm salt water (usually a teaspoon of salt to one glass) or two aspirin crushed in some water. Children should use acetaminophen or ibuprofen instead of aspirin because of the possible link to Reye's syndrome. Hydrogen peroxide may also be effective. Besides gargling (which not everyone can do easily), other recommendations for sore throat relief include:

- drink plenty of liquids, especially hot ones like tea.
- avoid acidic drinks that could increase irritation (which counts out the lemon juice remedy).
- suck on hard candy or lozenges. The ones with mild anesthetics temporarily numb the pain, but sucking on anything will stimulate saliva and moisten the throat.
- use a vaporizor in the room to help keep the air moist.

It's always a good idea to check with the doctor about the possibility of a strep infection, which can be treated best with antibiotics.

Prunes Help Prevent Constipation. *True*

Now, wait a minute ,you say, this is no wives' tale, this is fact. Well, not exactly.

In an article for the *Harvard Health Letter*, Dr. Stephen Goldfinger reports that the medical research community has come up with limited support for the efficacy of prunes in the treatment of constipation. Trouble is, there hasn't been a whole lot of research done in this area, and much of what has been done has not been published.

Some fifty years ago a study was conducted at he University of California in San Francisco which found that diluted prune extract stimulated contractions of rabbit intestines. This indicated that more than just the fiber in prunes was at work! There must be an additional, active chemical ingredient. Studies in the 1960s and in 1987 at Boston University School of Medicine confirmed that prune juice was one of the most potent stimulators of intestinal fluid output.

What holds the medical community back from 100% endorsement of prunes? Simply that this mysterious active ingredient has not yet been isolated and identified. The closest anyone has come was at the Harrower Laboratory in St. Louis in 1951, when researchers found a compound resembling oxyphenacetin, an agent that at one time was widely used in commercial laxatives.

Later research at the Sun Diamond Growers and The University of California at Davis failed to isolate such a compound. More investigation is in order, but the topic is obviously far down the list of scientific curiosity. These days everyone wants to know if the healthful properties of wine have been verified. (See *Red Wine Is Good For You*)

So, what's the verdict on prunes? This is not just another OWT. Prunes and prune juice do contain some ingredient that helps stimulate intestinal flow, and they supply fiber that is strongly recommended for regularity. Many doctors recommend prunes and fiber over commercial laxatives. But like everything else, moderation is advised in prune use.

An Apple a Day Keeps the Doctor Away.   *Not True*

For starters this is a misnomer. These days, nobody has to keep a doctor away—they never come. Doctors don't make house calls. The correct phrasing of this should be "An Apple a Day Keeps *You* Away From the Doctor."

But, does any rational person actually believe that apples keep you healthy. Well, maybe, but with a whole bunch of qualifiers.

For instance: "An Apple a Day Will Keep You From Getting the Little Annoying Everyday Sicknesses Like Flu or the Common Cold."

Well, the Nobel prizewinning Dr. Linus Pauling promoted the idea that high amounts of vitamin C can prevent colds, and the controversy over this has been raging ever since. But where does the apple stand in relation to other fruits in the delivery of vitamin C? By comparison to citrus foods— oranges, grapefruits, lemons—apples do not come out too high. In fact, nutritionists rank cantaloupe, guava, papaya, berries, broccoli, green pepper, tomatoes, spinach, collard greens, potatoes, asparagus, and parsley above apples as a rich source of vitamin C.

Okay, let's try fiber. After all, we could say that "An Apple a Day Will Keep Constipation Away." There's no question that doctors and nutritionists all strongly recommend a good daily intake of dietary fiber—especially from fruits, vegetables, nuts, and seeds—as the sure path to regularity. Research also indicates that fiber may help in preventing colon cancer, diabetes, and heart disease.

But once again, the apple trails behind the pack. The American Health Association rates baked beans, wheat germ, kidney beans, navy beans, lima beans, and bran-rich cereal higher than an apple. Although, when eaten with the skin, it is considered as good a source of fiber as other fruits.

When it comes to more serious disease, such as cancer, there is absolutely no indication that apples are at all beneficial. What has made recent headlines is BROCCOLI! Studies over the past few years have statistically shown that people who eat regular, *moderate* amounts of cruciferous vegetables have a lower incidence of certain types of cancer. Now, researchers at Johns Hopkins University

School of Medicine have isolated a specific chemical in broccoli, called sulforaphane, that causes a significant increase in some of the body's protective enzymes that help guard against malignancies. Both microwaving and steaming methods of cooking leave the chemical intact.

So it's... "Broccoli Every Day May Keep Cancer Away."

The bad news for those, like George Bush, who simply can't stand broccoli, is that there are no plans to produce the chemical in pill form for painless consumption. The good news? Other cruciferous vegetables, including brussels sprouts, cauliflower, and kale, as well as some noncruciferous ones, like carrots, also contain high concentrations of sulforaphane.

In "Meals That Heal," a segment on CBS News, some other foods received attention as having possible benefits for a variety of conditions. Cherries and raspberries were highlighted for osteoporosis; grapefruit, oranges, and yes— broccoli—for relieving arthritis pain; bananas for decreasing blood pressure when under stress; licorice for ulcers; and passion fruit for insomnia.

So we have to pity the poor apple. After all these years and all that glory, it appears to be a rather ineffective little fruit.

Perhaps the proverb should be, "An Apple a Day Makes a Delicious Non-Fattening Snack, and You Get Some Fiber, a Little Vitamin C, and Potassium Into the Bargain." By the way, biting into an apple also helps clean your teeth—so we can also say, "An Apple a Day Keeps the Dentist Away!"

Hair of the Dog, the Ultimate Hangover Remedy.   *Not True*

One of the funniest moments on the hit TV Show, "Northern Exposure," was when Marilyn, the Native American secretary, offered a "hair of the dog" to the very hungover Dr. Fleishman. He made a terrible face, spit it out and asked, "What was in that?" She replied, "Hair of the dog."

That was carrying things a bit far, because the expression is really "the hair of the dog that bit you" and refers to giving the "hungee" some of the same booze that did him in. We asked a number of people from the medical community and from the world of folklore about the origin of the expression, but the best explanation anyone could venture was that it comes from olde England in her merry days.

Hangovers are really a terrible form of retribution for an evening of fun, much worse than we actually deserve. The worst part about them is there really isn't much that can be done except wait for the effects to wear off. But we've been trying for centuries, all the way back to Beowulf and the boys in the mead halls.

In researching cures for hangovers, we seemed to find as many different remedies as people asked. Which leads us to believe that nobody has a definitive answer. One thing is for sure, not one expert mentioned having another drink.

When nobody has a definitive answer it usually means that it has not been decided exactly what a given phenomenon is. And that seems to be the case with hangovers. We know what drunk is. Alcohol affects the brain when you have been drinking, and it gets there through the bloodstream. It also causes dehydration and depletion of vitamins like B, minerals like salt and potassium, and amino acids. But what causes the hangover?

A popular theory says the hangover is actually a withdrawal reaction. If that's the case, then the brain gets hooked on the alcohol in record time. According to Dr. Mack Mitchell of the Alcoholic Beverage Research Foundation, in just a few hours of drinking, the cells in the brain physically change. When the alcohol is all burned by the body and none follows, these cells go into withdrawal. In addition, alcohol causes the blood vessels in the head to swell, and this too can be the cause of the headaches, dizzy spells, and nausea.

Getting back to the "hair of the dog," it would seem that if the withdrawal theory is valid, then some ingestion of alcohol would give some relief, and there are people who swear that it does. The only problem is that unless you are going to continually ingest alcohol, this solution only prolongs or postpones the inevitable hangover.

The most sensible thing is to understand that the hang-over will run its natural course, and you will recover eventually. The idea then is to make life bearable, induce sleep if possible, and shorten the recovery time. If you remember how the alcohol affects the body, it's easy to see how the various "hangover remedies" have come into being.

One such remedy, *raw egg in tomato juice*, more than likely provides a quick fix of proteins that house amino acids, while the tomato juice helps reverse the dehydra-tion. Today, with salmonella rampant in raw eggs, you don't even want to think about this one.

If you can eat a mild meal (no fat or fried food) and keep it down, that's the quickest route to recovery. You'll be replacing everything the body has lost, and adding sugars which burn away the alcohol faster. If you can only nibble and sip, then make sure you get fructose (honey or fruit juice), salt and potassium (bouillon or other soups are best), and carbohydrates (crackers, rice, potatoes), for the depleted amino acids. Drink lots of water, and take a painkiller such as ibuprofen or aspirin as you would for any headache. The old standby, an icebag on the head, probably works by constricting swollen blood vessels.

Then there's *coffee*, drunk black and strong. Is there any benefit, or does it just give you the double whammy of a hangover *and* caffeine-jangled nerves? The fact is that coffee also aids in constricting those swollen blood vessels, and if taken in moderation (two cups), may reduce the headache.

Which leads us to another OWT...

Black Coffee Sobers You Up. *Not True*

This is one of the most common notions associated with drinking: If you can drink enough strong, black coffee, you'll sober up. It's often served at parties before people drive home, and offered free on New Year's Eve at highway stops. While it's true that caffeine may help relieve a hangover, and it may help a person stay awake, it does not lower the alcohol content in the body. So what you basically have is a wide-awake drunk, still very dangerous behind the wheel. Better to drink a lot of fruit juice and wait until the sugar burns up enough alcohol.

Beer Before Whiskey, Pretty Risky.
Whisky Before Beer, Never Fear. *Maybe*

This sounds a bit like one of those nautical rhyming tales, but we never found anything that traced it to the early sailors. The contribution, in fact, came from an old college friend who remembered this adage as holding her in good stead through countless frat parties.

My husband said that, in the Army, there were many, many theories about what and how to drink without getting drunk. Probably as many theories as there are ex-GIs. None of them seems to work very well. A neighbor, a chiropractor, swears by vitamin A. He believes he could drink all night without getting drunk if he stoked up on vitamin A first.

But, I digress.

Getting back to the optimum sequence of beer and whisky, we checked with the Alcohol Research Foundation. No one there had even heard of it, but on purely physical grounds, the first reaction was that the theory was "ridiculous." Alcohol is alcohol and it's the quantity that gets you drunk, not the order in which it is imbibed.

But after thinking it over a minute, someone suggested there could be some benefit in drinking the whiskey first. One could drink beer after beer without feeling drunk, then have some whisky, and end up with a dangerous amount of alcohol in the system.

But, if you started with whisky, chances are you wouldn't have that many because the awareness of the alcohol content is so much stronger. Then, if you had a beer or two as chasers, the chances are you would not have consumed as much alcohol.

You might even get happy faster without actually consuming as much alcohol as you would have if you started with beer.

But it's only speculation, and I, for one, would never mix beer and whisky anyway. Red wine is my drink, because...

Red Wine Is Good for You.   *True*

For generations, the French have been the authorities, not only on making red wine, but drinking it. Besides being pleasurable to the palate, red wine is considered essential in maintaining good health and strength. Several French friends remember being given red wine as children when they were sick, and being allowed wine diluted with water at meals. In certain areas of Northern France, it was common to give cranky infants a bottle of diluted red wine to help them sleep. Of course, alcohol is *not* recommended for children, no less babies. Several years ago the French government and health professionals became concerned about childhood wine consumption and a public campaign was mounted to discourage the practice.

So it's not surprising that French researchers have taken

a serious interest in determining if there was any scientific basis to the health claims for wine. Studies completed last year at the Hospital cardiologic in Pessac reported that drinking red wine, did in fact, seem to significantly reduce the amount of "bad" LDL (low-density lipoprotein) cholesterol—the kind that clogs arteries. At the same time, red wine increased the level of "good" HDL (high-density lipoprotein) cholesterol—which may protect arteries by cleaning out fatty deposits. For those of you who prefer white wine, I'm sorry to convey the finding that it was only the red wine that had a beneficial effect on cholesterol levels.

A possible explanation came from additional research by plant scientists at Cornell's College of Agriculture and Life Sciences. They succeeded in isolating a natural chemical in grapes, named resveratrol, which may be the critical substance. It's strongest in the grape skins, which are removed when making white wine. Interestingly, Japanese researchers have also identified resveratrol as the probable active ingredient in ancient remedies used for centuries in China and Japan to treat many different blood disorders. I recall that my mother-in-law was advised by her doctor (not Chinese) to drink a daily glass of red wine for her anemia, because it contained iron.

Last, there is also evidence that many red wines contain protein, which makes them food.

Now don't take all this good news about red wine as an excuse to sip your way through a bottle a day. Just because a little is good for you, doesn't mean a lot is better...moderation is the key word. And keep in mind that some medications shouldn't be mixed with alcohol in any amount, so always check with your doctor.

For those of you who can drink wine, and would like to conduct your own study, it's worth noting that out of thirty wines tested by the Cornell researchers, red Bordeaux was found to contain by far the highest amounts of reservatrol.

This was the same type of wine used in the French study. *A votre santé!*

Use White Wine to Remove Red Wine Stains. *Not True*

With all the recent publicity about the benefits of red wine, health-conscious Americans have started drinking more red wine at dinner—with the inevitable result. Last week, I watched skeptically as a friend used white wine to remove red wine stains from a valuable antique linen tablecloth. She had heard "somewhere" that it really worked, and the spots did seem to be lighter. But after the area dried, there were new, even larger, blotches from the white wine. No question, this is a real OWT.

Professor Herb Barndt, of the Philadelphia College of Textiles and Science, classifies all wines as causing the same type of stain since they all contain alcohol, fruit, and sugar. In his handy book *How to Remove Spots and Stains*, Professor Barndt recommends the following method for wine removal (test first on an inconspicuous area for color loss or damage):

"Sponge off stain with cool water. For washable fabrics, stretch the stained area over a bowl, pour salt over the stain, and pour boiling water through the fabric from a height of twelve inches. If the fabric can't take boiling water, pour salt on the stain and moisten. Let stand, then scrape the salt off, and rinse. If these methods are too harsh for the fabric or it is non-washable, use an oil solvent. If any stain remains, apply a vinegar solution (half water), and rinse."

The use of salt and cool water does seem to support the more common notion that *Club Soda Removes Wine Stains.* This certainly is more practical as immediate first aid during a dinner party than the boiling water procedure. But be sure to use club soda, not seltzer, since the latter is usually salt-free.

And here are two final axioms from Professor Barndt that are worth remembering...

Never Use Heat on a Sugar Stain!
Never Use Soap and Never Iron a Fruit Stain!

If You're Chilled, Have a Shot of Whisky to Warm You Up.   *Not True*

One of the most puzzling things to me was this familiar western scene. A rider, hot and dusty, comes in off the trail, pushes through the swinging doors, and bellies up to bar. "Ah'm parched, got a terrible thirst," he croaks. "Gimme a shot of whisky!"

Yuk! Can you believe it? Whisky, to quench a thirst...especially when you're dying of heat?

Far more believable is the idea of the trusty St. Bernard, bounding up to a stranded and freezing mountaineer, with a cask of brandy to warm the insides and provide sustenance for the cold trip down the mountain.

So totally logical is the idea of warming oneself with alcohol—the proverbial "Hot Toddy"—that probably ninety out of a hundred adults will seek out a bar or a flask to take the chill off. Alcoholic warmer-uppers like "Glühwein" and hot buttered rum are a traditional part of cold weather sports.

The fact is that alchohol does initially warm you up when you're cold. A shot of booze will increase the flow of blood to the skin and give you an immediate sensation of warmth. But, experts agree, it doesn't last very long, and can leave you feeling more chilled than before.

This leads to your taking another shot, getting another

short-lived burst of warmth which is quickly lost to the air, which leads to another, etc. In the end, you are not only cold, but in varying states of inebriation, and in danger of hypothermia and frostbite.

The correct solution is to drink hot, non-alcoholic liquids. Soup, tea, cocoa, coffee, hot cider, or even plain hot water. Also hot food if it's available. If there is no way to heat liquid, have it anyway to prevent dehydration which can aggravate chills and frostbite.

When you're back in a nice warm place, have had a hot bath and a good dinner, and are sitting by the fire, that's the time for a small snifter of very old cognac.

3

If You're Carrying High, It's a Boy and Other Expectations for the Next Nine Months

Until the last few hundred years or so, pregnancy and childbirth have been shrouded in awe and mystery. It's no wonder that countless old wives' tales were born and passed along for generations in an attempt at linking cause and effect. For example:

Predicting the Gender of the Baby   *Not True*

If you carry high, it's a boy.
If you carry low, it's a girl.
Hold a needle on a thread above the abdomen: If it swings clockwise it's a boy; Counterclockwise, it's a girl.
Hold a long piece of cotton over the abdomen: If the cotton moves back and forth, it's a boy; If it hangs straight, it's a girl.
Compare the mother's age at time of conception with the year of conception: If both are even or odd, it will be a girl; If one is even and one is odd, it will be a boy.

And the list goes on and on. The last one dates back to the Aztecs, who were known to be advanced mathematicians. But not that advanced. It's curious that with all the curiosity and speculation that surround determining a baby's gender, no one has done any definitve studies to test these theories. An obstetrician friend confided that he has been conducting his own informal observations on the high and low hypothesis, but he's not about to publish any findings and "leave myself open to professional ridicule!"

Another obstetrician said the current fad among her pregnant patients is to check the baby's heartbeat, believing that the speed (fast or slow) gives an accurate determination of the baby's gender. This idea is so scientifically unsound, maintains this doctor, it's not even worth keeping track of the predictions and results.

Current tests for genetic abnormalties—amniocentesis and chorionic villus sampling—make it possible to detect if you're carrying a boy or a girl. Sonograms have become a relatively routine part of fetal monitoring during pregnancy, and a sharp-eyed technician can often spot the physical clues. Still, it's up to the parents to decide whether they really want to know beforehand. For many, especially the grandparents-to-be, the guessing game is part of the fun.

Don't Raise Your Hands Above Your Head, the Umbilical Cord Will Strangle the Baby.
Not True

Of course, there's no way the position of your arms can possibly affect the position of the umbilical cord, which is securely enclosed, along with the baby, inside the uterus. This one was probably started by old midwives who were afraid of retribution when this tragedy occurred, preferring instead to pass the blame along to the poor mother. What's remarkable is that even in this century, my mother remembers being warned against doing anything that required raising her arms, like hanging curtains.

If You Have Heartburn When You're Pregnant, the Baby Will Have Lots of Hair. *Not True*

I'll never convince my mother this one isn't true. She suffered from constant heartburn throughout her pregnancy, and I was born with long dark hair.

However, as any doctor will point out, heartburn is caused when the stomach contents back up into the esophagus. Chocolate, smoking, caffeine, and fatty foods can worsen the condition, as can lying down. My mother did have to spend the last few months in bed to prevent premature labor, so perhaps that was the source of the heartburn.

In any case, this is a problem confined to the gastrointestinal system, which is separate from the heart and the uterus. So I refuse to accept guilt...my long hair was purely a coincidence!

If You Give in to Your Craving for Strawberries, the Baby Will Have a Strawberry Birthmark. *Not True*

Doctors stress that it's important for pregnant women to eat a balanced diet and that includes plenty of fruit. So if you crave strawberries, you can indulge yourself without guilt. There's no scientific basis linking any foods, eaten while pregnant, with any kind of birthmark—gynecologists say they are genetically determined.

The so-called "strawberry" birthmark usually fades during childhood, even though it may get larger during the first year. However, disfiguring "port wine stains," usually on the face, are birthmarks that do not fade. Fortunately, the recent development of pulsed yellow dye lasers allow treatment of port wine stains, even in newborns, without scarring.

You Can't Get Pregnant as Long as You're Nursing.
Maybe

With the modern choices available in contraception, it's unlikely that any mother is going to take the risk of following this particular piece of advice. If it appears to work at all, the usual explanation is that a new mother, especially when she's up in the middle of the night nursing the baby, is simply too exhausted even to consider sex.

But, surprise of surprises, this is one old wives' tale that's really true—and the reason has nothing at all to do with fatigue.

For thousands of years and even today among some cultures, breast-feeding has been an effective method of birth control, with children spaced three to four years apart. A study of pregnancy rates among Orthodox Jewish mothers, who used no artificial birth control, supported findings from underdeveloped countries.

However, what *is* essential is that the child be fed exclusively with breast milk—no supplemental bottles of formula and no solids—completely on demand.

Doctors explain it this way: First, when an infant nurses, there is a reflex reaction that directly inhibits the brain from releasing the hormone that allows the pituitary gland to make LH (luteinizing hormone) which is necessary to trigger ovulation. Menstruation is also delayed. Second, sucking on the breast also stimulates the pituitary gland to release the hormone prolactin. High level of prolactin in turn inhibit the pituitary's release of the hormone LH.

The levels of prolactin are directly related to the length of time the child nurses, as well as the frequency. Since giving supplemental bottles and/or solid food reduces the amount of time spent nursing, the levels of prolactin are also reduced, allowing ovulation.

So if you're willing to have your baby breast-feed as often as he or she is hungry, with no schedules and no supplements, you might consider asking your doctor about using this method of birth control. Of course, you may be too tired for sex anyway.

Once a Caesarean, Always a Caesarean. *Not True*

No one knows for certain if this notion dates back to Roman times, when this procedure was first named after the emperor Julius Caesar, who, as you may have already guessed, came into the world via a surgical incision. Until a few years ago, the assumption in the United States was that having once delivered by C-section, one must deliver any other infants the same way because of the risk of rupturing the uterus during the birth process. Naturally, this rule contributed to the rising number of caesarean deliveries, now at 25 percent of all births nationwide.

In other countries, vaginal deliveries after C-sections were quite common and the dictum began to ease during the last decade. The obvious advantages include lower medical costs and faster recovery. Selected women who had had only one low transverse incision were allowed to attempt a "trial of labor" for a vaginal delivery. Studies, conducted at large medical centers with routine fetal monitoring and standby surgical teams, showed successful results. It seems this OWT really has become an outdated notion, in most cases.

However, two reports in the June 1991 issue of *Obstetrics and Gynecology* raise some concerns over the increasing popularity of the practice. They estimate that one in every one hundred subsequent vaginal births has resulted in uterine rupture and serious complications for mother or baby. Dr. Roy M. Pitkin summed it up in an accompanying editorial: "The message seems clear: Many women with previous caesareans can be delivered vaginally, and thereby gain substantial advantage, but neither the decision for trial labor nor management during that labor should be arrived at in a cavalier or superficial manner."

You Can't Get Pregnant If You Have Sex Standing Up. *Not True*

When I mentioned this OWT to a friend, he recited this little ditty from his youth...

> "In days of old,
> When knights were bold,
> And girls were not particular,
> They all stood up against the wall,
> And did it perpendicular."

Today, girls *are* particular, especially when it involves an unwanted pregnancy. Unfortunately, one out of ten teenagers becomes pregnant, in part due to misinformation like this. Of course, the idea of vertical birth control is ridiculous to most adults, but it appears to be born again with each generation that enters adolescence...along with another popular misconception, pardon the pun, that *"you can't get pregnant the first time."*

While working on a television show with teenagers, I was quite surprised to find out how many really otherwise "cool" teenagers place their trust in the perpendicular. It's a belief that seems to be based on an exaggerated faith in the power of gravity, plus an ignorance of biology.

Sperm, the reasoning goes, cannot swim up, and therefore can never even make it into the vicinity of the egg, let alone hang out long enough to commit any unwanted fertilization. Ergo, safe sex.

This is only wishful thinking. Intercourse is intercourse, and the sperm will not simply give up. They will do what they're designed by nature to do...no matter what you do, or how you do it.

So if we're talking contraception, forget perpendicular.

4

....And Speaking of Sex

Masturbation Causes Insanity, Blindness, Hair on Your Palms, and Stupidity, etc.   *Not true*

My husband remembers that a typical teenage joke was to say: "I heard that masturbation causes hair to grow on your palms," and watch everyone sneak a furtive look at their hands. Even today, it would probably still have the same effect.

Down through the ages this completely natural activity has taken a very bad rap, spreading untold guilt and fear among generations of young people. Back in the 1940s the *Boy Scout Handbook* gave strong warnings against the practice. Yet doctors reassure that masturbation is a normal part of sexual development and doesn't harm the body, or mind. Children, even in infancy, soon discover that touching their genitals "feels nice." It doesn't mean they are "oversexed" (no such thing) or will become sexually active at an early age.

So there's absolutely no reason to instill guilt in a child. On the other hand, what can an embarrassed parent do when a young child, quite naturally, masturbates in public?

Psychologist Penelope Leach says to calmly explain that touching one's "private parts" is something that is best done in private. It should be kept on the same par as other social no-no's like picking one's nose.

Don't Have Sex Before Competition, It Saps Your Energy. *Not True*

For years, this was a common admonition from athletic coaches; some still use it before the "big game." The fact is that sexual intercourse, like masturbation, does not cause weakness. If anything, it probably helps to reduce tension and anxiety, thereby improving performance.

5

If a Newborn Baby Smiles, It's Only Gas and Other Parenting Proverbs

When a Newborn Smiles, It's Only Gas. *Not True*

It's not a very charming way to describe those first smiles that parents wait for with so much expectation. But, unfortunately, gas is much more likely to generate a grimace or cry than anything resembling a smile. According to *The Growing Years*, a guide from the New York Hospital-Cornell Medical Center, even "These first smiles, (that appear as early as six weeks of age) are not in response to another person; they aren't social smiles, but are indications of contentment."

Not to worry, however. Babies soon begin to smile at "anything vaguely resembling a face," an indication of beginning socialization. By the age of three months, babies smile at parents in preference to other people, which doctors point out is "a crucial development because it indicates that the infant is responding selectively and specifically" and attachment is taking place. So go ahead and make all the silly faces you want. You may feel like an idiot, but isn't a baby's smile worth it?

I'll pass on a tip I got from Dr. T. Berry Brazelton that's sure to elicit a response from even a six-week-old. I tried it last month with a friend's baby. Just stick your tongue in and out, very slightly, making whatever sounds you can. The baby will soon start moving her tongue, smiling, and making "conversation."

Drink a Glass of Beer or Wine Before Nursing the Baby. *Not True*

Texts as far back as first-century India recommend wine for the nursing mother, while many European countries have touted beer as useful in increasing the flow of milk. Now, there's no doubt that a little alcohol can relax a frazzled mother, but what effect does it have on the baby?

Some research done with nursing mothers has shown that drinking one beer, or its equivalent in other booze, actually has a negative effect: babies eat less, not more.

Since nearly everything a mother eats or drinks gets passed along in the breast milk, the alcohol may be sedating the baby.

Physicians strongly advise against drinking alcohol when nursing, or giving a baby alcohol in any form. And that includes "gripe water," an over-the-counter potion containing about 5% alcohol commonly used in Britain or former British colonies for relieving a baby's indigestion. Although the Food and Drug Administration regards the product as a drug and has not given approval for sale in the U.S., it has been imported illegally from Britain.

Drinking lots of fluids is more effective in producing an adequate flow of breast milk. The recommendation is two to three quarts a day of water, juice, or milk.

However, would you like to know what really makes a baby nurse better? *Garlic*!

The American Academy of Pediatrics noted that a recent study by the Monell Chemical Senses Center found that when a mother ate garlic, one to two hours before nursing, there was an increase in the perceived intensity of the odor of their milk. The infants stayed attached to the breast longer and ingested more milk when the milk smelled like garlic.

No accounting for the tastes of babies!

Solid Foods Will Help a Baby Sleep Through the Night.   *Not true*

Unfortunately, the only people helped by this advice are baby food manufacturers. If it really worked, there wouldn't be so many weary new parents longing for just one unbroken night's sleep.

Until the 1980s infants were started on solid food, usually cereal, at about four weeks of age. The seemingly defenseless child would sit, propped up in a corner of an infant seat, while you patiently spooned the food into his little mouth. Then, through a phenomenon known as the "extrusion reflex" (a self-protective mechanism that prevents infants from swallowing anything but liquids), he would push the food back out. In some frustration you scraped it off his chin, tried again, and maybe eventually, some food ended up inside the baby.

Not only is this aggravating process a waste of time, and baby food, but the American Academy of Pediatrics warns that young infants might have difficulty digesting and absorbing the food that does go down. Their digestive systems are really set up to handle breast milk or formula, not solids, during the early months. Another danger of starting solids too soon is that it may make a baby more prone to allergies since at this point, the intestinal tract doesn't yet have the immunologic defenses against foreign proteins.

What is the best age to start giving solids? The Academy recommends waiting until a baby is at least four months old, preferably six months.

Tell that to your mother-in-law who says you're starving her grandchild.

A Baby Should Always Sleep on Her Stomach, So She Won't Choke If She Spits Up....A Baby Should Always Sleep on Her Back, So She Won't Suffocate. *Not True*

The choice of old wives' tale you hear on this matter depends upon which side of the Atlantic you're on. In Europe, infants are put down to sleep on their backs. But in the U.S. the custom, even in many hospitals, is to place infants on their tummies. This can make for some real battles, especially if you have a "cross-Atlantic" marriage.

Until recently, most pediatricians considered either position equally acceptable for a healthy baby. However, in April 1992, the American Academy of Pediatrics released the recommendation that "healthy infants, when being put down to sleep, be placed on their side or back." What led to this statement?

During the 1970s, the infant sleeping position in the Netherlands reportedly changed from predominately supine (on the back) to predominately prone (on the stomach). An abrupt increase in SIDS (Sudden Infant Death Syndrome), also called "crib death," was noted soon afterward. SIDS strikes about 1.5 per 1,000 infants. In the mid-1980s, after studies noted a relationship between SIDS and the prone position, the lay press and a few investigators in other countries began to advocate side or back sleeping positions. Subsequent to this change, very preliminary reports from New Zealand and the United Kingdom noted decreases in the incidence of SIDS by more than 50 percent.

What about the concern over the possibility that a baby might spit up and choke if he were on his back? In the same statement, the Academy noted, "Despite common beliefs, we discovered no evidence that aspiration (choking) is a more frequent complication in infants lying supine (on their backs) when compared to other positions." They also point out that "aspiration is a very rare cause of infant death." The new recommendation does not apply to babies with symptoms of gastroesophageal reflux. Of course, it's best to check with your own doctor or pediatrician.

Despite the new recommendation, the Academy goes on to stress that "the actual risk of SIDS when placing an infant in a prone position is still extremely low." After the age of four or five months, most babies decide for themselves which position they prefer, and parents shouldn't go running in to turn a baby over if he likes sleeping on his stomach.

What's most important is for a young baby to always sleep on a firm, flat infant mattress, without pillows, large stuffed animals, or puffy comforters in the crib. That way, she can easily move her head to find breathing space. Surfaces like thick sheepskin rugs, soft foam mattresses, cushions, water beds, and bean bag cushions may seem comfy, but infants can suffocate when these beddings trap exhaled carbon dioxide.

When a Baby Is Teething, It's Normal to Run a Fever. *Not True*

No! Teething does not cause fevers or make a baby more susceptible to colds. A fever is a sign of an infection, and should be checked out with your baby's doctor, especially if it's above 101 degrees F. for a day.

Other things—drooling, a slight loss of appetite, problems sleeping, increased diaper rash, and crankiness—can be blamed on teething. Dentists say the process really isn't as painful as adults think it is...and I'm sure no one actually remembers. But there are some ways to soothe the gums. Try a teething ring with gel that can be chilled, or gently massage the gums with a damp gauze pad. Don't rub with ice which could damage the gum's covering. And never cut the gums to help the teeth come through...that *is* painful and can cause infection.

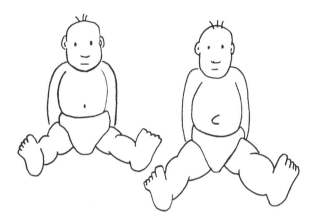

Whether the Baby's Belly Button Is an "Inny" or an "Outy" Depends on How the Doctor Cut the Umbilical Cord.

Not True

"Innies" and "outies"...doesn't that bring back memories from childhood? Of course, no one ever thought or even cared about the cause, it was just something fascinating to compare. In truth, the obstetrician can't be blamed either way. The position of the cut makes no difference: what does determine the shape is the same thing that shapes the baby's fingers...heredity.

My husband's grandfather had a wonderful explanation of belly buttons in general. He was a baker and drew his grandchildren's attention to the indentation at the center of a rye bread. "This was made," he said, "by the baker when he poked the bread to see if it was done." That's what God does, too, to tell if each new baby is ready to be born.

Whether you are an inny or an outy depended on your state of doneness when you got poked. I guess you can call this one an "old baker's tale."

A Cat Will Steal a Baby's Breath. *Not True*

Adult cats often look like they're guilty or up to no good, which is the source of the expression "the cat that swallowed the canary." Even the most fanatic cat lover will admit that most cats seem to really enjoy making, or getting into, trouble. So, when there's a helpless little baby around, it's easy to look at the family tabby and see a real green-eyed monster prowling the nursery.

But do they really suffocate babies, "steal their breath"? The answer is "No." This is one time where poor cats have gotten a bum rap. The belief probably arose from the unfortunate phenomenon that used to be called "crib death," when a perfectly healthy infant mysteriously dies while asleep. Cats love to curl up to anything warm, and it's likely that if they were found in the crib, they took the blame. The condition is now known as SIDS or Sudden Infant Death Syndrome, but there's still no definitive answer as to the cause.

Many pediatricians do agree that for other reasons, like allergies, it may be a good idea to keep the cat out of the nursery.

Don't Pick a Baby Up Every Time She Cries. She'll Get Spoiled…It's Good for a Baby to Cry, It Exercises the Lungs.   *Not True*

This is sort of two old wives' tales in one, and the combination has created generations of howling children and guilt-ridden parents. My mother said she wore ear plugs for my first few months because my screaming was so upsetting.

Fortunately, doctors and psychologists are now reassuring parents that there's no way a young baby (up to six months or so) is capable of scheming to manipulate helpless parents with the idea, "If I cry long enough and loud enough, I'll get picked up." According to respected pediatrician Dr. T. Berry Brazelton, "You can never spoil a baby with too much love and attention. Your baby is helpless, and when she needs you, she communicates in the only way she can, by crying. You teach her trust and security with lots of loving attention."

Studies have also been done on the effects of picking a baby up even when she's not crying. By six weeks of age, babies who had been carried around and cuddled an extra hour or two a day were observed to cry less. This was particularly evident during the late afternoon and evening "fuss periods." Crankiness and crying were actually cut in half.

86

However, there is one condition that all the attention and cuddling in the world may not help: colic! Opinions differ on what causes colic, defined by doctors as "severe abdominal discomfort in a young infant." Desperate parents will try anything: music, rocking, swaddling, and even marathon walking sessions. When nothing works, at least not for very long, it's easy to see how parents become frustrated and guilt-ridden. Once colic is diagnosed, it's important for parents to remember, "It's not our fault, it's nothing we did, and it's nothing we didn't do."

The good news is that colic doesn't last all that long: babies usually outgrow the condition by their third month.

Babies Are More Sensitive to Cold, So They Need to Be All Bundled Up. *Not True*

The way some parents encase their children in protective bundling, you would think they were taking a walk on the moon. These little "astronauts" are so wrapped in layers against the cold air they are barely able to wiggle their fingers. Why all this over protectiveness? Well, many parents truly believe that babies, especially in the first few months, are less able to cope with cold weather.

Not True, says the American Academy of Pediatrics. A 32-degree temperature, or below, is no colder to a baby than to an adult. So there is no reason to dress your baby any more heavily than you dress yourself. They do cite one area of exception: the baby's head. Because it's proportionally larger in terms of body area compared to an adult's, a baby can lose correspondingly more heat through his head. So, it's okay to go heavy on the hats.

The same rule about dressing applies indoors as well. If you don't need to wear a heavy sweater, neither does your baby. Just remember, an overbundled baby won't complain, he'll simply perspire and break out in prickly heat. So prevalent is this scenario that pediatricians say they treat more cases of prickly heat in the winter than in the summer.

If your baby is getting cold, he'll let you know by crying and turning a bluish mottled color. And, don't try to go by the feel of the child's hands or feet. They're generally a little colder than the rest of his body. Check the little tummy for a better indication of the baby's temperature.

If You're Not Quiet, You'll Wake the Baby.   *Not True*

This frequent warning is often given to older children in the family and doesn't do much in the way of encouraging a positive attitude toward a new sibling. Is it really necessary? Doctors say it all depends on the baby. Even newborns are individual: some are aroused easily by the slightest noise, while others can sleep through a Super Bowl game. I had one of each.

For most young infants, a normal level of conversation is fine, so there's no need to whisper. A sudden noise or shout may cause the baby to react a little, but not fully wake up. Many desperate parents have also found that monotonous sounds of vacuums, fans, lawn mowers, drills, engines, etc., actually help put a cranky baby to sleep. The only problem is that the baby is likely to wake up as soon as you stop. I soon learned, after wearing the carpets out, it works just as well to tape the sound of a vacuum cleaner and play it as long as needed!

The Later a Baby's Teeth Come in, the Better They'll Be.   *Not True*

This notion may have been started by mothers (more likely grandmothers) whose offspring were slow in cutting their first teeth. It certainly makes a good conversation

88

stopper when someone starts bragging about how soon *her* grandchild's teeth appeared. Unfortunately, it is the hapless babies who innocently find themselves in endless competition—even within the same family—to be the first to turn over, teethe, crawl, walk, talk, get out of diapers, etc.

In the long run, it doesn't make any difference who's early or late. Pediatricians keep reminding anxious parents that children develop according to their own timetables, and that includes teething. Usually, the first tooth breaks through the gum at around five to six months of age, but some infants are born with a tooth. Other children may not get that first tooth until after their first birthday. The quality of the teeth certainly isn't affected by the timing.

Baby Teeth Aren't Important Anyway.   *Not True*

Now this misconception probably originated as the perfect comeback to the above OWT. However, instead of being harmless, this belief could create serious problems. The American Academy of Pediatrics states clearly that "Baby teeth, or primary teeth, help children chew food, speak clearly, and retain space for the permanent teeth that start to erupt at around five or six years of age."

The Academy stresses the importance of taking good care of baby teeth by cleaning them daily as soon as the first tooth appears (with a piece of damp gauze or cloth), and by getting proper amounts of fluoride (even before teething begins). Since the amount of fluoride in local water varies, it's best to check this out with your baby's doctor.

The most harmful thing you can do is put a baby to bed with a bottle of milk or juice—and that's exactly what many parents do. When these infants fall asleep, they can end up with a small pool of liquid in their mouths. The sugar in the milk or juice combines with bacteria to eat away at their teeth, causing what's called "baby bottle decay." This can also happen to a toddler who carries around a bottle of milk or juice all day and sucks on it frequently as a pacifier.

Pediatricians strongly recommend that if a baby must go to bed with a bottle, make it plain water.

You Have to Warm a Baby's Bottle.   *Not True.*

This dictum was most likely laid down at the beginning of the century when formulas were developed for use in bottle feeding. Before then, a mother either breast-fed her baby, or hired a wet nurse. Obviously, the reasoning went, since breast milk was served up at body temperature, bottles needed to be warmed to the same degree. Or else, I was warned by certain well-meaning relatives, "The milk will chill the baby's tummy."

What no one took into consideration was that while breast milk is available immediately in a warmed state (one of the many advantages of breast-feeding), bottles need to be heated, tested, then usually cooled a little. All this takes time, during which you have a hungry baby screaming at the top of his lungs—especially frustrating at the 3:00 A.M. feeding.

Around the same time my second child made the switch from breast to bottle, I started doing research for a book I was writing, *The Complete Guide to Preparing Baby Food*. More than a little short on time, I asked my pediatrician if it was really necessary to warm the formula. His answer was, "There's no real reason, it's just tradition." I checked some more and found that some hospitals didn't warm bottles even for newborns. As for the "chilled tummy theory," a doctor pointed out that the milk would be warmed anyway during the trip down. The recommended test of "shaking a few drops on the inside of the wrist" was used only to determine if the formula was too hot.

The revelation that there is no "right" temperature went right into the book, along with the advice that you could serve formula direct from the fridge. Over the past twenty years, the book has become a best-selling classic, with the latest revision out just last spring. In all that time, no one has ever written in to criticize cold formula. However, if your baby is already accustomed to warmed bottles, it is important to lower the temperature gradually, or he may object.

When shocked grandparents object, you can offer the additional rationale that cold formula allows less chance of spoilage. But if someone does insist on heating bottles, be careful of using the microwave. The disposable bottles should never be "nuked" because the warm milk can continue to expand until the liner breaks. Infants have been scalded that way. A rigid plastic or glass bottle can be heated, but be sure to shake the bottle to distribute the heat evenly and always test the temperature.

After all this discussion on bottle feeding, I'd like to end with the following recommendation from the American Academy of Pediatrics:

"The benefits of breast-feeding are so numerous that pediatricians strongly encourage the practice. Human milk is nutritionally superior to formulas for the content of fats, cholesterol, protein, and iron."

Newborns Can't See. *Not True*

One of the most touching moments is when your newborn infant looks intently at you with such clear eyes. Then someone says: "You know, she can't really see you."

Well, there's no need for disappointment. Research has indeed confirmed new mothers' conviction that babies, right from birth, can see very well, at least up to twelve inches away. Interestingly, that's the usual distance between a nursing baby and the mother's face. It's nature's way of helping the bonding process. Dr. T. Berry Brazelton has observed that infants can recognize their mothers' faces by the time they're two weeks old. For fathers, they take a little longer.

These findings also impact on the way newborns' eyes are treated. For years, it's been routine hospital procedure to use silver nitrate drops soon after birth to help prevent serious infections. However, silver nitrate is very irritating to the eye and can blur the infant's vision. The American Academy of Pediatrics and the National Society to Prevent Blindness have approved the alternative use of the antibiotics erythromycin and tetracycline. They're less irritating, and more effective against chlamydia infections. Discuss this with your doctor and the hospital well before your baby's arrival.

What about colors? Does it matter to the baby if the nursery is pale pink, blue, or shocking red? The answer from child development experts is, "Yes." They found that infants respond better to bright colors—like red, blue, yellow, and green. Surprisingly, large patterns of black and white, especially checkerboards, also catch their attention. As parents, we tend to think that babies should have restful environments, hence the traditional pastel decor. Obviously, they prefer visual stimulation.

Sit a Baby Up After She Eats, and She Won't Spit Up. *Not True*

One of the least endearing attributes of young babies is their habit of "spitting up." It happens just when you're least expecting it, usually when you, or the baby, are freshly dolled up in clean clothes. My younger daughter preferred waiting until my mother-in-law or some other relative was cuddling her. The usual comment was either, "You didn't burp her properly," or "Why don't you sit her up after she eats?"

Now, I knew I was doing a pretty good job as a "burper," and I was already propping her up in an infant seat to let gravity help keep the meal down. So why was it still coming up? One answer may be she was simply eating too much, or swallowing air during feeding. However, some recent studies have shown that sitting a baby in a upright position may instead make the condition worse by increasing the pressure in the stomach. The current advice is to place a baby on her stomach with her head slightly elevated by raising the head of the crib mattress (remember...no pillows!). Too late to help me, but it's certainly worth a try.

Teaching a Baby to Swim Helps Prevent Drowning.

Not True

Here is another OWT of recent origin, one that can lead to disaster. With the proliferation of backyard swimming pools has come a tragic increase in the number of infants and small children who suffer permanent injury or death from accidentally falling into the pool. In hope of preventing drowning accidents, parents started giving or enrolling their young children in swimming lessons. It's true that even babies can learn to swim a few strokes, but that doesn't mean the child can be considered drownproofed or water-safe. Instead, it can lull parents into a false sense of security.

The American Academy of Pediatrics say there is "little justification for infant swimming programs" and has issued a statement clearly advising, "Infants less than age three or four should not participate in swimming programs." They also point out that although infants usually hold their breath instinctively when immersed, they continue to swallow water. "This water may be absorbed into the bloodstream in quantities great enough to produce hyponatremia (too little sodium in the blood), which can lead to seizures several hours after the swimming class."

Young children may also be more prone to viral and ear infections if they spend a lot of time with their heads in the water. The national YMCA guidelines stress that children under three should not be forcefully submerged or dropped into the water.

I wish I'd known all this when I dunked my older daughter, Jennifer, in a pool when she was six months old. She held her breath all right, but came out screaming and wouldn't go near the water for the next two years. Smart kid!

Children Need to Get Ten Hours Sleep a Night. *Not True*

Since I needed to wake up by 7:00 A.M. during elementary and junior high school, my mother simply counted back and set a 9:00 P.M. lights-off bedtime. It didn't matter whether or not I was sleepy. Millions of wide-awake children are still put to bed at specific hours because "You need your sleep."

Of course, one can legitimately argue that children do need to get enough sleep, but does "enough" really mean ten hours? It all depends. The general advice from pediatricians is that the average six- to eight-year-old should get twelve ours a day; nine- to twelve-year-olds require ten to eleven hours; and thirteen- to fifteen-year-olds need nine to ten hours sleep. The critical word here is "average."

Children, just as adults, differ in their sleep requirements. Some can manage very well, even as toddlers, on eight hours or less a night. So instead of setting a firm time to go to sleep, doctors say parents should consider how the child wakes up. If she's wide awake and fresh in the morning, is alert in school and doesn't get tired and cranky during the day, she's probably getting enough sleep.

And just think of all the fighting that can be avoided by not forcing a child to try to sleep when he's not sleepy. In many families, this battle escalates into an issue that has nothing to do with sleep, but with power and control. When that happens, a child may continue to resist sleeping even when he is tired.

What if you're unlucky enough to have a child who can get by just fine with less sleep? Does that mean he can stay up until you go to sleep? Not necessarily. If you'd like a little peace, quiet, and free time at night—and what parent doesn't—you can still set a specific "bedtime." A child can read, play, sing, or anything he enjoys, so long as he's ready for bed and, preferably, in his room.

Don't Worry, It's Just Growing Pains. *Not True*

This advice brings little consolation to children who wake up at night with the feeling that someone is hitting their shinbones with a hammer. The pain usually disappears around age sixteen, after you reach adult height, so it seems to be valid. But is there really such a thing as "growing pains?"

No! Doctors agree that aching bones are not caused by the growth process itself, even though the condition is most prevalent among grade schooler and teens, especially girls. Lab tests and X rays show there's no abnormality in the bones, muscles or joints. But there's no agreement on what does cause the pain. Some possibilities include fatigue or changes in body structure.

The good news: a study at the University of Ottawa indicated that slow stretching exercises, morning and night, involving the long leg muscles can help prevent these nighttime pains. Again, doctors aren't sure why this seems to work. A gentle massage may also bring some relief.

Actually, there's no harm in using the term "growing pains." It's a concept that children can understand, and causes less anxiety than just saying, "no one knows."

Children Need to Wear Sturdy Shoes for Proper Support.   *Not True*

Most of us spent our first years clumping around in what my pediatrician calls "little white army boots." It's amazing we ever learned to walk. Made of stiff leather, with nearly inflexible soles, these high-top shoes were also very expensive considering that they were outgrown every few months. But concerned parents felt the money was well spent if it meant their children would grow up with strong straight feet.

Sorry to say, it was, and is a waste of money. Stiff shoes only inhibit the natural use of muscles, and toddlers have better balance and more stability when they walk barefoot or in sneakers. According to a recent review of research, the American Academy of Pediatrics concluded that "being barefoot is the best environment for developing feet." Even when there are seeming deformities such as flat feet, pigeon toes, knock-knees, and bowlegs, a respected pediatric orthopedist, Dr. Lynn T. Staheli, stresses that prescribing so-called "orthopedic" or "corrective" shoes is unnecessary. In the vast majority of cases, these problems correct themselves in time.

The only reason a child needs to wear shoes at all is for warmth and protection, usually when he's outdoors. The Academy says the most "effective footwear should be flexible, flat, lightweight, quadrangular (wide toes) and porous to allow air to circulate." Stay away from soles that are slippery (leather) or create excessive friction (some types of rubber) which may cause the child to stumble and fall. High-tops are good because they're less likely to slip off when a child is running. If the shoe or sneaker fits the bill, it doesn't matter how inexpensive they are, so there's no need to buy the most expensive.

Obviously, what's most important is proper fit. Shoes that are too small can create deformity, and if the shoe is too long, the child may be clumsy and awkward. Since you don't have to pay a lot, you can afford to buy the right size and throw them out when they're outgrown. If shoes are worn, and formed to the foot of one child, it's not a good idea to pass them on to the next. And you can still bronze those precious first baby shoes, even if they are sneakers.

Never Take a Sick Child Outside — *Not True*

This dictum passed into history along with doctors' house calls, and every mother nowadays knows it just isn't true. However, I still recall how shocked and indignant I was when the nurse told me to bring my three-month-old daughter (running a 102-degree fever) into the office. And in December, no less! I know I never went out, even in the summer, if I was running the slightest fever.

Besides being convenient for the doctor, there is an advantage in your going to the office. Keep in mind it's the

best place to do a proper examination and begin any necessary treatment. Obviously, there's no harm in taking a sick infant or child (dressed properly) outside even if it's for other reasons than going to the doctor.

6

Don't Store Food in Open Cans and Other Advice to Chew on

Don't Store Food in Open Cans, It Will Spoil. *Not True*

   I've heard this admonition all my life, but never had an explanation that made sense. After all, the inside of the can was sterilized before it was opened, so why not just cover the can and put it in the fridge? You save time and extra containers, which you don't sterilize anyway. Unless the can got pushed to the back of shelf and sat there for months, becoming a mold factory, I've never had open canned food spoil. Still, the warning has made enough of an impression so that I feel slightly uneasy whenever I ignore it.

   To get to the bottom of whether or not this really is an OWT, I went to the top source I could think of, the U.S. Department of Agriculture, and talked with the Supervisory Home Economist, Lois H. Fulton, M.S., R.D. She confirmed my heretical belief that storing food in the original can in the fridge does not cause it to spoil faster.

On the other hand, she did not recommend the practice. Why? Because the food is more likely to pick up an off-flavor from the can, even if it's covered. Now that's something that I can understand. In the recent book *Safe Food* the Center for Science in the Public Interest (CSPI) offers another reason for transferring food to another container. The authors point out that if lead solder was used in the seams of the can, the oxygen would help the lead dissolve and leach into the food, especially if it's acidic like tomatoes or citrus juice.

Lead, even in small amounts, poses a real danger because it builds up in the body. And it can leach into food even if the can is unopened. Fortunately lead-soldered cans are becoming rare in the U.S., but they are fairly common in imported foods, like mushrooms, fruits, fish, tomatoes, artichokes, and water chestnuts. CSPI recommends that you use only seamless cans or those with welded seams. You can usually tell if a seam is soldered by running your finger down the seam and checking for unevenness through the label.

Breakfast Is the Most Important Meal of the Day. *True*

My generation certainly grew up hearing, and believing, in this statement. Which doesn't stop most of us from rushing out in the morning fortified with only a cup of coffee and toast. However, in an estimated 40 percent of American families there isn't even an adult present in the kitchen to urge children to finish their breakfast. So, more children skip breakfast than any other meal. This is one adage that may end with this generation, unfortunately.

While no one has proven conclusively that breakfast is the most important meal of the day, it's at least of equal importance with lunch and dinner. Nutritionists warn that

your body burns the energy from food within four hours. Although you may use up less energy while you sleep, it's a long time until morning and you still wake up with the need for lots more fuel.

Some studies have shown that children who skip breakfast do less well in school. Besides lack of energy, we all know how tough it is to concentrate when your stomach's rumbling and you're counting hours until lunch.

In addition, a recent Canadian study suggests that skipping breakfast may increase the chance of a heart attack. It's been known that the incidence of heart attacks is highest in the first few hours after waking. According to the study, the blood protein (beta-thromboglobulin), which increases as blood cells prime themselves for clotting, averaged nearly three times higher in people who did not eat breakfast.

So, there's no doubt the importance of breakfast is more than just an old wives' tale. The problem comes in following the advice: How do you find time to make a proper meal and then make time to eat it?

The American Health Association recommends that

breakfast should supply at least one-fourth of the daily food needs. And it's important to include a variety of foods to supply energy until the next meal. Carbohydrates (bread, for example) can be digested in as little as thirty minutes; however protein (eggs, milk, meat, cheese) lasts longer, and can help you make it to lunchtime.

Many nutritionists say one answer is in expanding the common idea of what constitutes breakfast. Foods like pizza, peanut butter and jelly sandwiches, hearty soups, and fruit milk shakes are all perfectly acceptable and are more likely to be eaten by children. As for the question of preparation time, or lack of it, why not try recycling leftovers from the previous dinner. If, like me, you wake up in the morning barely capable of pouring cereal into a bowl, you can always spend a few minutes at night making a breakfast that only needs a quick nuking in the microwave, or can be eaten cold. Ever try leftover pizza right from the fridge? Not bad!

Carrots Are Good for Your Eyesight. *True*

After a visit with her grandmother, our younger daughter suddenly refused to eat carrots. Why? Bethany emphatically explained, "Nana said they would give me pointy eyes!" Upon further questioning, we finally figured out Nana had readily told her carrots would give her "sharp" eyes. An easy misunderstanding for a three-year-old.

We reassured her, and confirmed that, yes, eating up all her carrots would help her have good eyesight. Were we really just perpetuating an old wives' tale? Not exactly.

Vitamin A is necessary for maintaining normal epithelial tissue, which includes the cornea and conjunctiva of the eyes. It's also essential in helping the eye adjust efficiently to changes in the intensity of light, like going outside on a sunny day. A deficiency in this vitamin can cause eye problems, including burning, itching, and inflamed eyes. Of course, there are many, more likely causes.

So vitamin A is important for your eyes, and carrots are indeed an excellent source of carotene, a form of this vitamin. Other dark yellow vegetables (Sweet potatoes, melons) and dark green vegetables (spinach, parsley, etc.) also contain high amounts of carotene.

Another form of vitamin A is retinol, which can be obtained from liver, eggs, whole milk, cheese. It's obvious that by eating a varied diet, not just carrots, children and adults will get enough vitamin A.

And although vitamin A is necessary, it doesn't mean you should consume very large amounts or take supplements. Since this is a fat-soluble vitamin, excess amounts are stored in the body and can reach harmful levels. Too high a dosage of vitamin A has been implicated in some eye disorders and other health problems.

The bottom line: a moderate amount of carrots is essential for healthy eyes, but carrots or any other vitamin A food won't ensure 20/20 eyesight. I've been eating up all my carrots for years and I still need to wear glasses.

Mayonnaise Makes Food Spoil Faster.   *Not True*

For many kids, mayo can transform what they consider "yuck" into an edible sandwich. But every time my mother cuaght me spreading it on my childrens' school lunches, she warned…"You know, those sandwiches won't be in a refrigerator and the mayonnaise can make them spoil faster." I used it anyway since everyone seemed to survive, but I always felt slightly guilty that I was indeed increasing the risk of food poisoning.

It wasn't until years later, when I was researching a book, that I came across the statement that the acid (lemon juice or vinegar) in mayonnaise actually helps delay the growth of harmful bacteria and spoilage. I confirmed this revelation with nutritionists, doctors, and the U.S. Department of Agriculture. They did recommend the use of commercial mayo over the homemade type for two reasons: The acid content is higher and it's made with pasteurized eggs instead of raw eggs which often carry salmonella bacteria.

Even though this proved to be a real old wives' tale, it doesn't mean you should leave food unrefrigerated for hours, with or without mayo. All food contains bacteria and can spoil given enough time. But the mayo isn't the culprit. Of course, I'll never convince my mother and I still don't like mayonnaise on sandwiches.

Fertilized Eggs Are More Nutritious. *Not True*

Health food stores often make this claim, but the embryo in a fertilized egg is so small that it doesn't add any significant nutritional value to the egg.

Another common misconception is that a blood spot in the yolk means it's fertilized. No way. According to the American Egg Board, a blood spot is caused by the rupture of a blood vessel on the yolk's surface while the egg was being formed, or by a similar accident as the membrane travels down the reproductive tract. Should you toss it or cook it? These blood spots are really harmless, so don't even bother removing them. Unless you're like me—irrationally squeamish.

Here are a few more egg-cellent facts from the Egg Board about the new old wives' tales.

Brown Eggs Are More Nutritious Than White Eggs. *Not True*

Not so. The color of the shell has nothing to do with nutrition or flavor. It simply depends on which variety of hen is laying the eggs.

Raw Eggs Are More Nutritious Than Cooked Eggs
Not True

Absolutely not! However, they are more dangerous because a high percentage of eggs are contaminated by the bacteria that causes salmonella poisoning. Fortunately, it's destroyed by thorough cooking. Doctors advise against eating any raw of underdone eggs. No more sunnyside up, over easy, or loosely scrambled. That also eliminates drinking a raw egg in a glass of tomato juice as a hangover cure—ugh! Or is that just an old drinkers' tale anyway? (See page 59.)

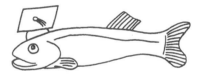

Fish Is Brain Food.
Not True

Ever watch the look on your family's face when you announce you're serving fish for dinner? Brrr! My husband complains that eating fish as a main course is like eating nothing. So the temptation to trot out the "brain food" story again is absolutely overwhelming. While a husband may be a more than a little skeptical, the kids are likely to swallow it...and the fish. Some old wives' tales are created and survive simply because they're useful.

Fish really is a healthful food. Most types are low in fat and high in protein, B vitamins, trace elements, and fatty acids, all important for normal brain development. It's smart to eat fish, but eating fish won't make you any smarter.

People have become more concerned about the possible chemical contamination of fish. The Center for Science in the Public Interest considers swordfish, striped bass, bluefish, catfish (unless farm-raised), and carp as the most likely to contain high levels of contaminants. The safest species are cod, haddock, pollock, small yellowfin and albacore tuna, flounder, sole, perch, Pacific halibut, sardines, herring, freshwater bass, trout, and lake whitefish.

It's also safest to eat only cooked fish. The center advises against eating raw fish or raw shellfish because of possible infection by bacteria and parasites.

You Can't Refreeze Food After It's Thawed.   *Not True*

Does this sound familiar? You're having a big barbecue for which you've been buying and freezing since last month. Now, when the chicken, hamburger, franks, chili, beans, and veggies are all thawed out, it pours buckets and half the people don't show—or they show up but half of them are on diets. Either way you're left with enough food to feed an army. But no problem. Since the coals are hot anyway, you can just cook all the meat and refreeze what you can't eat for future, no-mess, meals.

Here's an even worse scenario. You've been away for a week, and as you walk into the kitchen, you step into a puddle of water that's dripped from the freezer. Either the electricity went off, or the dog knocked out the power cord, or someone left something sticking out so the door didn't close tightly. Now you have a variety of foods, in various stages of thawing, with some of them completely limp and soggy.

What can you do if you're not able or willing to spend the next day cooking? After all, the warning *"Do not refreeze!"* is clearly stated on all those packages. Is the only alternative to throw the food out? Not necessarily.

This dictum was created by Clarence Birdseye back in the 1930s along with the first commercially frozen vegetables, probably as part of a smart marketing strategy. Freezers weren't as reliable in those days, and accidental defrosting was more likely. Refreezing can cause a loss of quality in taste and texture, so the cautionary label helped prevent complaints and couldn't hurt sales, since consumption was increased.

In fact, it is legal to refreeze commercially frozen fruits, vegetables and red meats sold in stores if they have been defrosted no more than a day and have been kept cold. But remember, there may be a loss of flavor and texture. Since there's no reason to buy refrozen foods, look for the warning signs—frost inside the package—just squeeze and listen for the "crunch", and boxes that are solid on the bottom with the space at the top.

Somehow, the public, along with food writers, came to interpret the package warning *"Do not refreeze"* as meaning that any food would spoil if it was refrozen. *Not so!*

Last year, the U.S. Department of Agriculture's Meat and Poultry Hotline received some fifty-five hundred calls from people who weren't sure about the safety of foods stored in their home freezers. I was one of this year's callers and got some eye-opening information about refreezing. The USDA advises that it all depends on how the food was defrosted, how long it's been defrosted, and its temperature. Here are some basic guidelines.

- First of all, if there is any off-odor, throw it away.
- Foods that are partially thawed and still contain ice crystals can be refrozen.
- Defrosted foods that feel refrigerator cold (about 40 degrees) can be refrozen within a day or so.
- Foods that have warmed above refrigerator temperature, that have been defrosted in the microwave, or in water, should not be refrozen because bacteria may have had time to grow. (That means those leftover hot dogs and hamburgers can go back in the freezer without first cooking, so long as they were kept in the fridge instead of left standing out on the kitchen counter or picnic table.)

The biggest revelation to me was that these rules applied whether the food was raw or cooked. I always thought that cooked foods, once defrosted, had to be eaten or thrown away. Of course, there may still be a loss of quality.

This is also true for raw fish and shrimp which are sold with the labeling "previously defrosted." The home economist I spoke with on the USDA Hotline said she was frequently asked about refreezing these foods. It's safe, but don't expect the same texture and flavor.

The USDA stresses that what's essential is to freeze the food correctly to begin with.

- For long term storage, be sure to use a wrap that's designed for freezer use, or rigid containers, and seal the package well. Paper, or thin plastic wrap, allows freezer "burn" (those dry brown spots) on food. The spots aren't dangerous, but it's a nuisance cutting them away.
- Freeze food as quickly as possible to maintain its quality.
- The best temperature is 0 degrees F. or lower. If you do lose power, a full freezer should keep food frozen

108

for two days, a half-full freezer for about a day, if you don't open the door.
- And it is true that a freezer uses up less energy when kept full.

One last word of advice: Try to label and date everything you put in the freezer. Non-commercial frozen foods tend to look alike. Every few months I defrost a collection of mystery packages just to find out what they are, and end up having to create some unusual meals.

Don't Eat Between Meals, You'll Spoil Your Appetite.   *Not True*

In terms of childhood aggravation and frustration, this all too familiar admonition ranks right up there with "Don't Read in Dim Light" and "Don't go Swimming After Eating." And it's just as unfounded!

To convince doubting mothers (and grandmothers), I went to the highest authority—the American Academy of Pediatrics—who sent me their guide *Right From the Start: ABCs of Good Nutrition*. It clearly states, "Snacking makes up an important part of childhood nutrition. Children must eat frequently because they have high energy needs." They advise two or three healthful snacks a day, planned "*between meals!*"

So what if a child eats less at dinner. It doesn't mean he "spoiled his appetite," only that he's not ravenous because he wasn't allowed food during the long stretch between lunch and dinner. Actually, it's mainly an American custom to save the largest meal for the last. In Europe and many other areas, the midday meal is usually the most elaborate and supplies energy needed for the rest of the active day.

The key word is "healthful" meaning full of nutrition, not

full of fat and sugar like potato chips and candy. Sure, these junk foods may supply energy, but no nutrition. Some good snacks are fresh fruits, raw vegetables, bagels, graham crackers, string cheese, turkey slices, peanut butter, pizza—anything you'd normally serve at meals, just in smaller amounts.

When you think about it, the practice of eating three meals a day is really designed more for adult convenience than children's needs. And doctors say it's a smart idea for adults to also eat smaller amounts, more frequently. There's even a new word that assuages any leftover guilt from getting caught with your hand in the cookie jar. instead of snacking, you can now say you're "grazing."

Storing Onions With Potatoes Will Make Them Sprout.   *Not True*

A friend came up with this adage which seemed to explain why the onions and potatoes I usually stored together under the sink would sprout in record time. Once again, I checked with Lois H. Fulton, Supervisory Home Economist with the U.S. Department of Agriculture.

She said she didn't know any reason why storing these vegetables together would cause sprouting, but they shouldn't be stored together anyway. Why? Because mature onions should be kept at room temperature, or slightly cooler, in loosely woven or open-mesh containers. However, potatoes should be stored in a dark dry place with good ventilation, at a temperature of about 45 to 50 degrees. High temperatures will speed up the sprouting process.

That's certainly a logical explanation for the garden that's usually growing in my under-sink cabinet. It was too humid for the onions, and too hot and humid for the potatoes.

Potatoes Are Fattening. *Not True*

These days, any informed dieter worth his fat knows very well this concept isn't true. One large potato contains 130 calories, no more than a serving of cottage cheese or tuna fish. Plus, it's free of fat and cholesterol, so long as you leave off the butter, sour cream, cheddar cheese, and gravy!

Yams and Sweet Potatoes Are the Same Vegetables. *Not True*

This is probably a relatively modern misconception, and one that seems to be very common. Back in the days when most people grew their own vegetables, I'm sure yams were very seldom confused with sweet potatoes. But is it really important to know they're completely different? The answer is "yes", because there's a real difference in nutritional value.

Nutrition Action, CSPI's health newsletter, points out that compared to yams, the orange-colored sweet potatoes are in the four-star category, especially when it comes to beta-carotene (a form of vitamin A). One medium sweet potato provides more than four times the U.S. Recommended Daily Allowance, while the poor pale yam contains none.

Many grocery clerks don't know the difference and the names are often used interchangeably. So ignore the signs over the bin, and try to remember that yams are longer and more cylindrical, with rough, scaly brownish or tan skin. Sweet potatoes are stubbier, and have tapered ends and smooth, thin skin that can range from orange to purple. You can rummage around until you find a tuber with a little skin scraped off. If the flesh is orange (which means beta-carotene), you have a sweet potato.

As for canned goods, I just checked the label on a popular brand I had on my shelf. In large letters, it clearly says "Yams." In smaller letters just below, it says "Sweet Potatoes." However, the list of ingredients on the side of the can does not list yams, only sweet potatoes, so that's the final word. I'm not sure if the manufacturer is confused, or just wants to cover all bases.

If you're still confused, don't worry. Most of the fresh "yams" sold in the United States are really sweet potatoes, and likewise for canned "yams."

A Watched Pot Never Boils. *Maybe*

This adage may be used to illustrate the need for patience when you're waiting for something to happen, but let's take a more literal approach. When we're talking about liquid boiling, *never* is an exaggeration. It is true, though, that picking up the lid, or leaving the pot uncovered, means that whatever is in the pot will take about 20 percent longer to come to a boil. You save time and energy when you cover a pot.

While we're on the subject of boiling, it would seem that a vigorous boil would be hotter and cook food faster than water that's barely boiling. Not appreciably! According to the book *Kitchen Science* the temperature is still within one or two degrees of 212F., the boiling point of water. A vigorous boil is more likely to adversely affect the texture and flavor of foods. On the other hand, all that turbulence may help keep pasta from sticking together (a little oil in the water also works well).

Finally, it's true that salt added to the water will raise the boiling point about one to two degrees F. This increases the time required to come to a boil, but decreases the cooking time. However, alcohol has a lower boiling point than water, about 175 degrees F. So if you decide to alter a recipe by

adding wine, remember to extend the cooking time by five to ten percent.

Whoever said, "It's as simple as boiling water?"

Cottage Cheese Is a Good Source of Calcium. *Not True*

I've written a lot about nutrition, but the answer to this one surprised me. Compared to other dairy products, cottage cheese is actually a poor source of calcium. During production, it loses 50 to 70 percent of the calcium initially present in the milk. Skim milk, non-fat yogurt, and Swiss cheese contain much higher amounts of calcium. As for non-dairy sources, broccoli, spinach, salmon, and sardines are high in calcium. This mineral is important in the diet at all ages because it helps prevent osteoporosis or "brittle bones."

Brown Sugar, Raw Sugar, Molasses and Honey Are Healthier Than Refined White Sugar! *Not True*

This is a new old wives' tale created in the health-conscious 1960s and 1970s. For hundreds of years, old wives never had a problem with white and refined sugar, basically because it was never available. They made do quite nicely with maple syrup, honey, molasses, and raw cane or beet sugar when that was handy. But are these sweeteners really better for you than white sugar?

Nutritionists all agree there is no significant amount of vitamins or minerals in any of these alternative sweeteners. So you can't ease your guilty sweet tooth with the justification that you're using "health foods." Honey has an additional problem in that it can cause the botulism toxin to grow in the intestinal tracts of infants. It should never be given to children under one year old.

These days, foods contain many other forms of sugar than just plain sugar, and these may seem, or be hyped to seem, as if they're more nutritious, but they aren't. Sucrose, fructose, high-fructose corn syrup, dextrose, invert sugar, lactose, and corn sweeteners are the most common ones you see on labels.

7

You Can't Get Too Much Sleep and Other Waking Thoughts

You Can't Get Too Much Sleep.   *Not True*

Not true. There's no benefit in getting more sleep than you need, and that varies among individuals. Yet, people can get into the habit of sleeping a specific number of hours, or they stay in bed because "it's good for you." Of course, there's no harm, but if you'd like a little more time during the day, try cutting back an hour of sleep for a few nights and see how you feel.

If it's of any help, the Better Sleep council reveals that the average person sleeps 7.5 hours each night. And the average number of hours a person spends asleep during a lifetime is a whopping 220,000!

You Can't Catch Up on Sleep.   *Not True*

Yes, you can usually catch up with one good long sleep, even if you've been burning the midnight oil for several

114

nights. And don't bother keeping count of hours of lost sleep—you don't have to make up every hour.

You Need Less Sleep as You Get Older.   *Not True*

Not necessarily. Adults generally need less sleep than children; however, the amount doesn't just continue decreasing with age. Older people, especially men, may wake up with frequent trips to the bathroom and then have difficulty in going back to sleep. It's also normal for sleep patterns to change as you get older and many people find themselves wide awake at 5:00 A.M. If you tend to get tired during the day, doctors advise adjusting to the new patterns by going to bed earlier or taking a nap during the day. Sleeping pills are not the answer.

A Nap Just Leaves You Feeling Groggy.   *Not True*

Not according to experts on sleep and attentiveness who say that an afternoon nap can refresh a person, especially if he or she has a stressful job. It could help reduce errors, at the same time increasing creativity and productivity. Research shows that people have natural circadian (twenty-four-hour) cycles that encourage us to sleep twice a day: in the middle of the night and the middle of the afternoon.

Psychologist Ernest Lawrence Rossi goes further in his focus on the body's ultradian (less than twenty-four-hour) rhythms which occur every ninety minutes. His recommendation: twenty-minute breaks every $1\frac{1}{2}$ hours to improve work performance, mood, and physical well-being. Tell that to your boss or teacher!

One Hour's Sleep Before Midnight Is Worth Two After.
Not True

False again. This old wives' tale was probably invented by mothers who couldn't wait to pack their teenagers off to bed.

A Little Warm Milk Will Help You Go to Sleep.
True

How many movies and plays have you seen in which someone offers the unsuspecting heroine "a nice cup of warm milk to help you sleep better?" Too often, the milk contains a sinister white powder that insures the drinker sleeps very soundly indeed, likely to be discovered dead in the morning, with the telltale cup smashed on the floor.

Assuming you trust the preparer and the warm milk is safe to drink, does it actually promote sleep? Or is this just an old wives' tale which mystery writers have found very convenient?

The truth is that milk *can* increase your chances of drifting easily off to sleep. It's rich in calcium which helps relax muscles, and is also a source of tryptophan, a protein that enables the brain to produce serotonin. This chemical, in turn, helps switch on the brain's sleep centers.

If you're like me, and can't stand the thought of warm milk, you'll be happy to know that cold milk works just as well. Though my husband insists that, warm or cold, the milk really needs a cookie to be effective.

Never Wake a Sleepwalker.

Not True

I hate to admit it, but sleepwalking has always seemed a little creepy to me. Like something out of the *Night of The Living Dead*, zombies walking with eyes open, arms outstretched. Other than seeing my young children in some state of half-sleep, I've never encountered a bona fide sleepwalker, and if I did I'd never even think of waking him or her. But, exactly what is supposed to happen if you do? The answer varies from one old wives' tale to another, with some warning the sleepwalker will become violent, while others are certain the result will be instant insanity.

According to sleep specialists like Dr. Richard Ferber, the

phenomenon of sleepwalking is a lot less bizarre or threatening and a lot more frequent than we think.

An estimated four million Americans sleepwalk regularly and as many as 15% of Americans believe they have sleepwalked at least once. It's even more common in young children—about one in six, usually boys—since sleep stages are still maturing. While there's no definitive answer as to why sleepwalking occurs, experts say it is definitely not a case of someone "acting out their dreams."

What can you do if you're one of the millions who live with a sleepwalker? One answer is to just let them walk. However, a person in this state may be unusually clumsy, and allowing the sleepwalker to make his or her way around the house might be potential hazard to china and furniture, as well as to himself. You'll be happy to know that you don't have to helplessly follow the sleepwalker around, trying to keep him out of trouble.

Doctors don't recommend shaking the wanderer awake, but it is perfectly all right to gently lead him back to his room and bed. If he happens to wake up, he won't go bonkers, but he may be surprised to find himself out and about. So it's important to calmly explain what happened— and no teasing in the morning! Sleepwalkers rarely remember their activities, and they'll deny ever getting out of bed.

To keep a sonambulist child from hurting himself, it's also a good idea to keep the bedroom clear of potential stumbling blocks and put a gate across the door. When sleepwalking becomes a problem for adults, try such simple advice as drinking less coffee before going to bed, or seek help from one of many accredited sleep clinics.

8

No Pain, No Gain and Other Rumors of the Workout Room

More people are running, jogging, lifting, and doing all kinds of exercise than ever before. Dieting and fitness are "in" and it's not surprising a new crop of OWTs have sprung up in the past few years. Like . . .

No Pain, No Gain.   *Not True*

They shout it at you from the TV screens, and in the gyms, and, if you're anything like me you want to shout back. "Pain? No exercise!" More of an Old Trainer's Tale than an Old Wives' Tale, it's a shibboleth that has acquired a patina of truth in a very short span of years. It is also why more than half the population of the United States still does not really exercise. We feel guilty, of course, but who, in their right mind, likes pain?

Drs. Peter and Lorna Francis (both Ph.Ds) have written a book called, *If It Hurts, Don't Do It*. Exactly my sentiments. But, if we "don't do it" when it hurts, will we derive any benefit? Is there gain without pain?

The answer is not a straightforward yes or no. It really depends on what exercises you are doing and why you are doing them.

You *should* exercise for health. It's a good idea to exercise for fitness. And you *can* exercise for strength and performance. Three different reasons demanding three different approaches, and two different answers to the no pain, no gain conundrum.

When exercising for health, a program of moderate exercise is in order. These are exercises that help lose and maintain weight; reduce the risk of heart problems through aerobic activities such as walking and swimming; maintain flexibility; and induce relaxation. When engaging in a program like this there is no reason whatever to do anything that causes discomfort, shortness of breath or pain. Just performing these activities in comfortable stages will bring about improvement in capacity.

Exercising for fitness requires more effort, more cardiovascular activity, more dedication, and should include stretching, aerobic training, and a program for building strength. Here again, there is no need to endure pain to achieve gain. It's okay to try pushing past a little fatigue, but when tired arms and legs start shaking uncontrollably, it's time to ease up. All of the above activities can be extremely beneficial without putting undue strain on your joints, ligaments, and cardiovascular system. Most important, by exercising within these painless guidelines, *there will be gain.* Your stamina and ability will steadily improve if you stick to your program. Even the strength training you incorporate in that program does not require pain to achieve results.

For those people who train for performance, the answer is different. These are people who are interested in building up a capacity for a specific sport, or simply building a very muscular body. Experts seem to agree that for developing specific muscles, there is benefit from the fatigue one feels as one reaches and pushes capacity, and not from excessive repetitions. However, the pain or "burn" must be still be mild and confined to the muscle itself. Great care must be taken not to tax the ligaments, the skeletal structure, or the cardiovascular system that supports those muscles. Research shows that injury rates are higher among the very fit; ignoring pain can almost guarantee an injury.

One of the most awful moments of my television sports viewing career occurred when I saw a weight lifter's leg snap under the weight he had hoisted. His muscular strength had achieved a capacity his skeleton could not support.

So, for serious trainers, mild fatigue pain in the muscle itself can deliver gain, but for the rest of us it's not necessary in order to get the benefit. Everyone who exercises, at any level, should keep in mind that pain is exactly what we have always thought it was...nature's way of warning us that we are abusing our bodies.

Muscle Weighs More Than Fat. *True*

Among the explanations heard when the scale doesn't budge or even creeps upward, this theory is the "heavyweight" champ, just edging out "heavy bones." People say they exercise and exercise but because the muscle they are building weighs more than the fat they are replacing, their weight remains constant. Are they right? Perhaps; This is not the whole story.

Partially because he wanted to know, and partially to get me to let up on him at dinnertime, my husband asked Diane, the very knowledgeable trainer at his gym, what she knew about the subject.

"It's like the old question of a pound of bricks or a pound of feathers," she answered. "Muscle is muscle and fat is fat and a pound of each is a pound of each." *But...* and here's the difference.

Muscle is more dense and will weigh more than an equal amount of fat, just like a brick will weigh more than a stack of feathers the same size as the brick. But how does that all relate to weight loss? Will a person who is exercising and building muscle actually gain weight? The answer is in the calorie intake.

Let's compare two people taking in two thousand calories per day, one working out, the other not. The workout will burn most of the calories while building muscle, so that person will lose weight. The calories taken in, but not used, by the sedentary individual will build fat.

However, if the person who is working out increases his or her intake of calories, then there will be less and less weight loss as they bulk up. They will be building muscle but not burning enough calories, and the extra calories will go to fat. This is a general rule and, naturally, the three different body types—mesomroph, endomorph, and ectomorph—will react to the rule at different rates.

When You Stop Exercising, Muscle Turns to Fat. *Not True*

This popular myth is perpetuated by the apparent frequency of gigantic football players and weight lifters turning into "the Blob" when their careers end.

Again, muscle is muscle and fat is fat. They are different tissues that cannot metamorphose one into the other any more than flax can be spun into gold. The sloppy ex-athlete is simply continuing, or increasing, his or her intake of calories without burning them off with exercise, thereby adding fat to the body.

The appearance of muscle turning into fat, and visa versa, is, however, another story and brings us to the next common saw...

You can Get Rid of Cellulite.   *Not True*

Some French marketing genius, no doubt lounging on la Croisette in Cannes sipping a glass of Byrrh and partaking of a zesty bowl of spaghetti bolognese, was musing on the lack of opportunities. Suddenly, his experienced eye noticed something...something both ugly and beautiful at the same time. Leaping from his chair, and knocking the spaghetti and wine onto his white linen trousers, he screamed the French word for "Eureka!" Looking, as Frenchmen sometimes do, at the thighs and backsides of hundreds of women, he had discovered, tucked beneath their suntanned skins, a motherlode of pure gold.

He had discovered what would become known as cellulite, one of the great myths of the twentieth century, or an "Old Advertisers' Tale."

We don't know for sure that it happened that way, but it could have. What we do know is that this designation and labeling of a purely natural phenomenon, occurring most often in women, gave birth not only to a billion-dollar industry, but a complete pseudo-science as well. There's even a "pinch test" that will cause a dimpling effect known as the "mattress phenomenon," supposedly a sign of the "disease."

In *The Skin Book*, the authors Drs. Arnold W. Klein and James H. Sternberg state clearly that "cellulite is an imaginary condition"...there's no such entity as cellulite itself. They go on to say that "studies have shown that 'celulite' is not actually a disease, but merely an anatomically normal irregularity, simply a result of the fact that fat deposits in the women's legs are different from fat deposits in men's legs." Men have crisscrossing connective tissue strands that keep the fat from forming in large chambers as it does in women.

Since their book came out ten years ago, this perfectly normal condition has spawned a gigantic network and substructure of institutions, clinics, "professionals," and folklore of technical expertise. Products by the hundreds, featuring miracle drugs, enzymes, etc., have been developed to be taken, injected, and rubbed into the "affected areas." Recommendations include massaging to break up the "cellulite," combating constipation, opening the blood vessels beneath the skin, getting rid of salt, staying off coffee and cigarettes, eliminating specific foods, deep breathing, and stress management.

Much of this advice will contribute to improving one's general health, but won't help to get rid of those ugly dimples—which women are obviously desperate to do—myself included.

So is there any hope? Drs. Klein and Sternberg confirm the accepted medical recommendation that only exercise and weight loss may help somewhat in reducing these fat deposits, and can forestall them if you begin early enough—female athletes simply do not have cellulite.

9

If a Dog's Nose Is Hot and Dry, It Means He's Sick and Other Clues to the Secret Lives of Pets

If a Dog's Nose Is Hot and Dry, He's Sick. *Not True*

We thought this rule of thumb was so obviously true that it wasn't even worth covering. However, the woman at Animals By Choice asked if we were going to say anything about the dog's nose.

Why? We wondered. Because, she said, it was one of the most flagrant examples of a commonly accepted fact that was dead wrong. A dry nose indicates nothing at all about a dog's health. It is only a sign that the dog has been inactive for a period. He has either been sleeping or resting.

The lesson from that is not to take anything for granted, no matter how obviously true, or false. Each common notion must be checked out. And that's why we asked this obvious question...

Always Mount a Horse From the Left.   *Not True*

Did you ever wonder what would happen if you tried mounting a horse from the right? You weren't about to find out, right? Given how big he was and how that big brown eye was watching your every move. If the left is where the horse wants you, the left it is, thank you.

But if you think about it rationally, from a safe distance of course, does a horse really know left from right? Does he care? Some friends thought it had something to do with side vision.

For the answer we turned to the folks at the Horsemanship Safety Association in Wisconsin. The bottom line is that horses really don't care, at least not instinctively. A horse can be mounted, as well as dismounted, from either side. However, if a horse is always mounted from the left, he learns to expect that and may react if approached from the right. In other words, it's an acquired response.

Steve Bennett, the Executive Director of HSA, explained that mounting from the left is a very old tradition, one he believes dates all the way back to the days of knights in armor with three- to four-foot swords.

Sword scabbards were usually worn on the left side, where predominantly right-handed warriors could draw them more easily. This bulky piece of equipment no doubt made mounting the horse from the right more than a bit awkward. If the knight wanted to mount on his scabbard side, he would have had to tilt backward, in forty or so pounds of armor. The resultant collapse and clanging would not have been cool, and that's to say nothing of all the fuss involved in hoisting him back into position.

Today, the logic for left-side mounting has disappeared along with the knights, swords, and scabbards, but the habit has continued. Mr. Bennett recommends that horses be trained to be mounted or dismounted from either side. But if in doubt about the horse's education, it's safest to stick to the left side. He also advised that new riders should be taught to disregard this OWT and mount from either side... provided the horse is willing.

By the way, another interesting tidbit to come out of the conversation with Steve Bennett was the origin of the expression, "getting one's goat." It seems that in days of yore, it was discovered that a race horse maintained a pleasant disposition if it had company in the stable. The perfect companion, it was found, was a goat, which is a docile, mild-mannered beast. What they had to talk about in those long, tedious hours is anyone's guess, but it did work.

Soon, nefarious types discovered that if one wanted to annoy or agitate the horse (especially before a race) one merely had to abscond with the goat. The subsequent loss of the race would also irritate the horse owner in a big way. Thus... "getting your goat" came to be equated with irritating or irking.

Barking Dogs Don't Bite. *Not True*

Some do, some don't.
According to the people at the SPCA of Westchester County in New York, you believe this one at your own risk.

Barking dogs can and do bite, both before and after they bark.

If a Dog's Tail Is Wagging, She Is Friendly.   *Maybe*

The dog that's barking at you may also have his/her tail wagging at the same time. Does this mean that this barking dog won't bite?

A spokesperson at Animals by Choice, a nonprofit organization also located in Westchester County in New York, said that your chances of safely approaching a barking dog whose tail is wagging are pretty good. The tail wagging usually means that the dog is happy, and not belligerent. But it's not a hundred percent certain; people have been known to be bitten by dogs who were wagging their tails.

Does Purring Mean a Cat Is Happy?   *True*

Well, the good news is that it does. Surprise! The purring a cat does is left over from the days of communication with mama cat, just like the kneading cats will do with their paws.

In kittenhood, cats use their paws to knead the mother in order to obtain milk from a teat. When happy or content they will retain this kneading as well as the purring. They will also use purring as a "love call" to their master or mistress when they feel affectionate. I won't even try to tell this to my husband. He, like most men, does not think cats are capable of affection and are only interested in people as sources of food and shelter.

10

The Full Moon Makes People Crazy and Other Weather Reports

Moon Myths... Tides, Sex, Sanity, and the Weather.

On the first evening after the dawn of civilization, primitive man looked up and there it was: the moon.

Fortunately we don't really have to imagine what he or she thought of this nearest celestial neighbor... legends, religions, folklore, and years of study have been documented and chronicled and we have enough information available for a life's work.

For instance we know that it didn't take early man very long to discover a correlation between the rising of the moon and the local tidal ebb and flow. And it was this power that placed the moon into the hierarchy of early religions, along with the sun, the wind, the rains and snows, and the seasons.

We will probably never know when man first noticed the hounds baying at (or in sync with) the full moon, or that his own romantic interests seemed to be aroused at the same time. However, there was enough connection between the rising of the moon and offbeat behavior for the words "lunacy" and "lunatic" to enter our vocabulary, *luna* being the Latin word for "moon."

Today, and for recent history, we understand that the moon's "power" is its gravity, or gravitational pull. We also understand that the moon moves around the earth in an elliptical orbit, bringing it nearer on a predictable timetable, and changing the way it appears to us.

Since the moon is smaller than the Earth, its gravitational pull is less and it cannot move the Earth itself (there is some debate on this) very much. But it can affect things on the earth, and what it does and does not affect defines the validity of some very familiar Old Wives' Tales.

The Moon Governs Tides. *True*

This is unalterable fact, so much so it cannot really be deemed an OWT. We only include it because it seems to be the proof that other OWT are true. For an explanation of this phenomena we turned to a very lucid piece of writing by Patrick Moore, director of the Lunar Section of the British Astronomical Association, and a prolific writer and lecturer. In his book, *New Guide to the Moon*, Mr. Moore explains the rather complicated variations of tides and lunar proximity, and although quite fascinating, it's too involved to get into here. But the very simple explanation is that the water heaps up as the moon passes near the various parts of the Earth, almost like a wave following a magnet.

The odd thing is that the water also heaps up on the opposite side of the earth at the same time. This is explained as either the result of the Earth being pulled away from the water by the moon's gravity, or the result of a total absence of gravitational pull from the moon on that side of the Earth. According to Mr. Moore, this is still under debate.

The Full Moon Makes People Crazy. *Not True*

Despite our words lunatic and lunacy, the word seems to be that this is simply not true. Patrick Moore went to considerable trouble to research this and found that the moon had no discernible affect on the behavior of human beings, nor any other land-based creature. But, Mr. Moore admits to a slight amount of prejudice since he spends a lot of time looking at the moon and doesn't really want to think his sanity has been affected.

Because of this, we turned to the American Museum-Hayden Planetarium in New York, to see if there was any later thinking on the subject. After all, human beings are about two-thirds water, so it would seem to be a logical assumption. Suzanne Chippendale, the planetarium's writer and producer, was happy to back Moore up. When asked why the moon's gravity can affect tides and not people, she explained that people were simply too small to be affected. In other words, there has to be considerable size and mass for all that gravity to matter.

So how did all this "lunacy" business start? There had to be some aberration connected with the moon. Ms. Chippendale has a rational response to that, too. It is simply the light from the full moon. The fact is that more light, especially in the days before we knew how to make our own light in ample quantities, caused changes in the behavior of all creatures, both on land and in the sea. People could be active under a full moon in a way they could not when there was little or no moonlight, and the same holds true for animals and fish who can use the extra light to find food. Which brings us to the next moon-related OWT...

We Are More Romantic, and Conceive More Babies During a Full Moon.   *Not True*

"By the Light of the Silvery Moon," etc., says it all, according to Ms. Chippendale. Full moons are romantic because they are pretty, and because of the light they deliver. Spooning in the moonlight is more fun in the same way that it's nicer to spoon in a rose garden than on a city street, but has nothing whatever to do with the gravitational pull of the moon.

Ms. Chippendale and Mr. Moore also agree on the "statistics" regarding conception during a full moon. They cite something that is the bane of all research: "a search for coincidences will always reveal them." In other words, it is easy to find proof that there is an increase in conception during a full moon, if you look for it. However, further research will reveal other jumps in conception rate that have no relation at all to a full moon. Both instances prove nothing.

The Full Moon Eats the Clouds.   *Not True*

Here is a weather-related old country adage that springs from the observed phenomena of the sky always clearing when a full moon rises. Although quite often true, these phenomena have more to do with the sun than the moon, as the sun can cause weather changes and it is generally believed that the moon does not. Moonrise occurs as the sun sets, and any clearing activity in the sky has to do with the setting sun and not the rising full moon.

A Ring Around the Moon Means Rain.   *True*

The soft and often beautiful "haloes" we sometimes see around the moon can indeed be precursors of rain. Again, we refer to the writing of Patrick Moore, who informs us that these rings are cased by the moonlight shining through ice crystals hovering at around twenty thousand feet. These ice crystals are part of a cloud called cirrostratus, known to mariners as "mares' tails." They are a high, wispy cloud that is very often a sign of approaching bad weather.

The moon can also look "watery" because it is seen through a lower and denser cloud, and this too, can mean a soggy day is in the offing.

Red Sky at Night, Sailor's Delight. Red Sky in the Morning, Sailors Take Warning.   *True*

This is really an old salt's tale that has come ashore and into the general vocabulary. But, is it true? And, why is it a rhyme?

My husband and I are recreational sailors and, quite frankly, we've learned this particular adage is a lot more reliable than those highly paid TV meteorologists. On one of our cruises between Martha's Vineyard and Point Judith, Rhode Island, we chose to believe the dead calm weather and the radio report, rather than the decidedly red morning sky. With full sails up, we got the ride of our lives.

In the days before sophisticated technology, seafarers, like old wives, built a treasure trove of collective practical experience...and their lives depended on knowing it well. Slow-moving and totally at the mercy of the wind and sea, they learned what every sky condition, wind change, and sea shape meant. Then, over the years, this collective knowledge developed into rhymes and couplets that even the most illiterate sailor could remember. It was a system they used not only for weather, but for many common chores and everyday practice aboard ship, and an extensive collection of these rhymes was part of every sailor's experience. They are very different from the wealth of superstitions that also went with the territory.

Unlike most of this collection, which dealt with conditions unique to the open oceans, these "Red Sky" couplets can apply on shore as well, provided the air is not over polluted. The explanation is simple. The colors of the sky are established by the refraction of the sun's rays through certain atmospheric conditions, including pollution. Normal refraction during fine weather and clear air singles out the color blue from the spectrum and sends it our way. As the sun goes lower in the evening, and the air is still clear, the refraction from this lower angle gives us the red sunsets which signal continued fine weather.

However, when the atmosphere begins to change, and moisture begins to filter in, the morning rays are refracted red, giving us our red sunrises. Time to break out the umbrella and galoshes.

Here's another couplet that often proves true...

> "Mackerel skies and mare's tails
> Make tall ships carry short sails."

I'm sure you can recognize this sight. The clouds described will look exactly like fish scales and horse's tails, and are situated very high in a lazy blue sky. But it's dead certain that, like the tall ships, you'd better get ready for some wind and storm.

And if you want to know if a summer squall is going to last or blow over quickly, just remember...

> "With the rain before the wind,
> Stays and topsails you must mind.

> But with the wind before the rain,
> Your topsails you may set again."

And, referring to the barometer, or "glass"...

> "First rise after low
> Foretells a stronger blow."

Finally, the ever-hopeful seaman entreats the seabirds:

> "Seagull, seagull, don't sit on the sand,
> It's never good weather when you're on the land."

Don't Stand Under a Tree in a Thunderstorm.

True

In case you're thinking "Of course, that's not an old wives' tale, it's absolutely true"—you're absolutely right! But judging from the speed with which most people run for shelter under the nearest tree, as soon as the skies open, they either haven't heard this warning or think of it as just another OWT. Unfortunately, thousands of people are injured each year by lightning.

The National Safety Council clearly explains: "Trees are tall and therefore attract lightning. Since wood is not a good conductor, an electrical current may jump from a tree to a nearby person before touching the ground." They recommend that if you are in a wooded area when a storm hits, stay at least six feet from any tree.

It can also be dangerous to be on hilltops and in open areas such as golf courses, soccer fields, and baseball diamonds—especially if you're holding metal objects like golf clubs, baseball bats, fishing poles, tennis rackets; or riding a bike, moped, motorcycle, farm vehicle, etc. These all make wonderful lightning rods, so get rid of them, or get off them immediately. If you are caught in the open, the

Council's advice is to "crouch low to the ground, with your hands on your knees." Don't lie flat on the ground because that increases your chances of being affected by electrical currents when the ground is struck. Sure, you'll be wet and uncomfortable, but alive.

The best idea is to get in the habit of keeping a "weather eye" when the skies are threatening. In almost all cases, you can see the towering thunderhead storm cloud formation approaching, and occasional lightning flashes, at least half an hour in advance, plenty of time to take shelter. Even when darkness makes it hard to see the sky, keep in mind that light travels much faster than sound. It is possible to estimate the distance in miles; just count the number of seconds between the lightning flash and the accompanying thunderclap, then divide by five. If the interval between seeing the flash and hearing the thunder becomes noticeably smaller, then the storm is moving toward you.

The Safety Council also points out "The most dangerous time to be caught outdoors is just before the storm, when dark clouds appear and your hair feels as if it's standing on end. You're being set up as a perfect lightning rod."

Talk about stupidity, I vividly remember one evening sailboat race. For half an hour, countless eyes in over thirty boats observed dark clouds, thunder, and sharply defined lightning bolts come closer and closer. But everyone hung in, with spinnakers flying, trying to reach the finish line before the storm. For once, it was lucky we weren't in the lead—that boat took a direct hit. Fortunately, most larger sailboats are grounded to handle lightning, and the only real damage was to all the electrical instruments.

Of course, water is normally a great conductor of electricity and the last place to be in a storm; that's why it's "out of the pool" at the first clap of thunder. Where is it safe? The Council says a metal-top car or bus, with closed windows, because the vehicle's frame will deflect the charge to the ground. The best place to take shelter is a large, lightning-protected or steel-framed building. However, since an estimated eighteen thousand homes in the U.S. are struck by lightning each year, here's some advice if you're at home during a storm.

- Unplug the TV set because the charge can travel down the antenna and cause the set to explode.
- Don't use the telephone or electrical appliances because lightning can also travel through phone lines and electrical wiring, giving a serious shock to anyone touching the receiver or appliance.

Now I realize this may be more than you ever wanted to know about lightning, but you never know when it may come in useful. At least you'll be able to recognize any real old wives' tales about electrical storms.